THE BEGINNER'S GUIDE TO
Windows 7™

- 📷 **Create Documents**
- 📷 **Burn CDs**
- 📷 **Email & Internet**
- 📷 **Security Features**
- 📷 **Parental Control**

**SUSAN HOLDEN AND
MATTHEW FRANCIS**

summersdale

THE BEGINNER'S GUIDE TO WINDOWS 7

Summersdale Publishers Ltd
46 West Street
Chichester
West Sussex
PO19 1RP
UK

www.summersdale.com

Printed and bound in Great Britain

ISBN: 978-1-84953-108-5

Substantial discounts on bulk quantities of Summersdale books are available to corporations, professional associations and other organisations. For details contact Summersdale Publishers by telephone: +44 (0) 1243 771107, fax: +44 (0) 1243 786300 or email: nicky@summersdale.com.

Acknowledgements

Microsoft product screenshots reprinted with permission and copyright © of the Microsoft Corporation. Windows 7, Windows Media, Hotmail, MSN, Microsoft, MS-DOS, Windows, Aero, Windows Live Mail, Windows Live Essentials, and Internet Explorer 8 are registered trademarks or trademarks of the Microsoft Corporation. All images used are the property and copyright of Microsoft and the use of such is not meant to convey any endorsement of this book. The use of any third party material within Microsoft screenshots does not imply any endorsement or connection between Microsoft Corporation and said third party.

© Acer is the trademark and logo of Acer Inc.

The screen shots of © Trees for Life – Restoring the Caledonian Forest, (www.treesforlife.org.uk) are reproduced with kind permission of Sales & Development

Manager, Jane Beaton. Our thanks go to Jackie Perkins and Zoë Julian of Churchtown Farm, Isles of Scilly for allowing us to use screenshots of their website (www.scillyflowers.co.uk).

The keyboard illustrations are reproduced with kind permission of Edward Lewis, SEO of Consultants Directory (www.seoconsultants.com). All images used are the property and copyright of the companies concerned and the use of such is not meant to convey any endorsement of this book. The use of any third party material within Microsoft screenshots does not imply any endorsement of this book.

Thanks also to Lesley Kristian, Sheila Todd, Pamela Griffiths, Shirley Penn, and J. D. Seargeant. For keeping us on track, we are indebted to our superb, patient and hard-working editor Lucy York, and our meticulous copy-editor, Stephen Watson.

Dedicated to Mark Seargeant
and kidney donors everywhere

In memory of Zach

Contents

Chapter Seven:
Personalising your Computer.................................144

Chapter Eight:
The Ease of Access Center...................................177

Chapter Nine:
The Accessories Folder...187

Chapter Ten:
Computer Security and Maintaining Privacy......211

Chapter Eleven:
The Internet...260

Introduction

Whether you are a complete beginner or just new to Windows 7, this book will help you discover some of the most frequently used features of Microsoft's latest operating system. Emailing, browsing and searching the Internet, working with images and playing music are just some of the subjects covered. There are chapters on keeping your computer secure and well maintained and ways to personalise Windows 7 in your own individual style. It also includes some of the basic and most common word processing elements needed to create documents. Windows 7 comes with free software called Windows Live Essentials and there are details on how to access and download this optional package. Discover 'Live Mail' the email program that now incorporates the easy-to-use Calendar and get to know 'Live Photo Galley' that gives you increased versatility in working with digital photos.

Microsoft Windows 7 is very user-friendly; we hope that you will find this book to be a useful, and friendly, companion. Long and detailed technical explanations are not included! Each chapter is divided into sections, and the text is in straightforward, bite-sized, easy-to-follow steps that we hope will lead to immediate success.

Chapter One:
Setting up Windows 7

There are six editions of Windows 7: Starter, Home Basic, Home Premium, Professional, Ultimate and Enterprise. The Starter edition is only available preinstalled on netbooks and small PCs. It provides just the basics and is useful for emailing, connecting to the Internet and creating Word documents. You cannot install it yourself, although it can be upgraded to another edition. Home Basic is aimed at emerging markets such as South America and Asia and is not available worldwide. The Professional and Enterprise editions are primarily for businesses or large companies. Ultimate combines all the features of all the editions.

Home Premium is the edition most commonly on offer for home computing and is the edition upon which this book is based.

Section 1:
Installing Windows 7

Using a New Computer

Assemble your new computer and ensure that all the cables are correctly attached – you should check the manufacturer's instructions that came with your purchase. Press the power button on the CPU: the computer will start and the screen will display a request to create an Administrator Account (see Section 2). If an Administrator Account has been created for you by the computer store or manufacturer, the screen will require you to log in (see Section 3) with the password that you have been given. Once you have logged in using this password, change it for one of your own (see Section 4).

Upgrading an Existing Computer

If you are upgrading your existing computer to Windows 7 then insert the Windows 7 CD. It will complete a check to see if your computer has a large enough memory and is fast enough: if your computer is able to run Windows 7, it will start to install the software. You will need at some point during the set-up to enter the number on the CD – this is to verify that you are using a genuine Microsoft CD. You will also be asked to create a user name and password. Follow any further instructions as they appear on the screen.

If your computer is able to carry Vista, then you will probably be able to upgrade it to Windows 7. If you have a computer which is running XP (or earlier), then it's a good idea to take it to a good computer centre and ask them to assess whether it has a large enough memory and is fast enough before you purchase the upgrade.

Section 2:
Setting up User Accounts

As part of the setting-up process you will be required to create a user account with a user name – this can be your own name or whatever you choose – and a password.

Choosing a Password

Your account password is important for the security of your personal files and information stored on the computer, so choose a strong one including numbers as well as letters. Remember that passwords are case sensitive. Whether you are upgrading or using a newly installed edition of Windows 7 we strongly recommend that you create a Reset Disk which can be used in the event that you forget your password and are unable to log in (see Section 7).

User Accounts

There are three different types of User Accounts: Administrator, Standard and Guest.

The Administrator

In first setting up Windows 7 you will have created an **Administrator** account which lets you configure the computer, change settings, set parental controls and install programs. The Administrator has complete access to the computer but will be required to give password confirmation when making changes that affect all other users. Confining such alterations to the Administrator provides additional security for the computer and its users. This book assumes that you are the Administrator of the computer and have access to all parts of Windows 7.

Standard Account

A **Standard** user account allows a person to access their own personal files and folders but not to alter security settings or settings that affect other users. They can be created for each person who uses the computer and should be password protected – this is strongly recommended – in order to safeguard personal files and information.

Guest Account

The **Guest** account is already set up and can be used by people who do not have a standard account and who are not the administrator – i.e. a user who has one-off or infrequent use of the computer. It's not password protected and the user cannot access the personal files of the other users. The Guest account can be turned on or off.

Section 3:
Logging In

1. Click on the User Name, click in the text box and type in your password.
2. Click on the arrow or press enter on the keyboard.
3. If your log in is successful Windows 7 desktop will open.

Failed Log In

1. If your log in has failed, it's most likely that you have typed your password incorrectly.
2. Retype your password; it's case sensitive, so remember to use capitals and lower case as in the original password (if using lower case, check the capitals lock key is off).
3. If log in still fails, click on the link 'password hint' (A in Fig. 1) to help you remember.
4. If you are still unable to remember your password, click on the link **Reset password** (B). You will need to use the Reset Disk in order to complete the process.

5. If you do not have a Reset Disk you will need to use the Administrator account to reset your password.

6. If you are the Administrator and have forgotten the password you will need to seek the help of a computer professional. You may need to reinstall Windows 7.

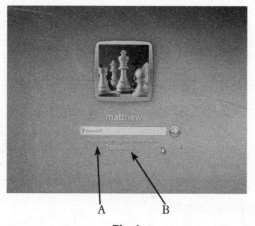

A   B

Fig. 1

Section 4:
Making Changes to your User Account

1. Click on **Start,** then on **Control Panel**, and in large or small icons view (A in Fig. 2) click on **User Accounts** (B).

2. The **User Accounts** window allows you to change your account password, picture and name.

Change or Set your Password

1. Click on **Change your password** (D).
2. Type your current password in the first text box, your new password in the second text box and confirm it in the third text box (A in Fig. 3).
3. Click on the link **How to create a strong password** (B) to get an idea of what to choose.
4. In the fourth text box type in a password hint – something that will help you remember, in case you forget your password.
5. Click on the **Change password** button (C) and the new password is set.

Change your Account Picture

1. Click on the link **Change your picture** (D in Fig. 2).
2. Select a picture by clicking on it and then click the **Change your picture** button.

Change your Account Name

1. Click on the link **Change your account name** (D in Fig. 2).
2. Type in a new name and then click on the **Change Name** button.

Section 5:
Managing Other Accounts

An administrator account is able to manage the other accounts on the computer. This is especially useful if adults and children share the same computer as it allows parental controls to be set.

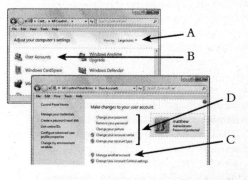

Fig. 2

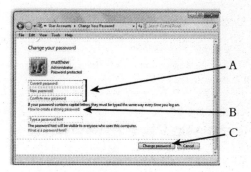

Fig. 3

1. Click on **Start**, then on **Control Panel**, and in large or small icons view click on **User Accounts**.
2. Click on **Manage another account** (C in Fig. 2).
3. Click on the account name that you wish to manage.
4. Click on whichever item you wish to change and follow the very easy instructions.
5. If you wish to set parental controls see Chapter Ten, Section 19.

Adding a New User Account

1. Click on **Start,** then on **Control Panel**, and in large or small icons view click on **User Accounts**.
2. Click on **Manage another account**.
3. This new window shows existing accounts. Click on **Create a new account** (A in Fig. 4).
4. A new window opens; decide whether you wish to create a new **Standard user** account or another **Administrator** account. Click the relevant option button (B).
5. Type in a name for the new account in the text box (C).
6. Click on the **Create Account** button (D).
7. A new window shows the new account holder's name along with the other user names.

Turning on the Guest Account

1. Click on **Start,** then on **Control Panel**, and in large or small icons view click on **User Accounts**.
2. Click on **Guest** (E).
3. Click on the **Turn on** button to activate.
4. To turn off the guest account, return to the guest account page and click on **Turn off the guest account**.

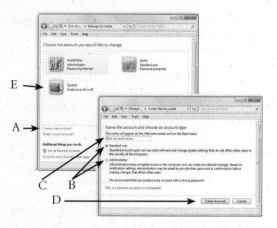

Fig. 4

Section 6:
Switching Users

To switch from one user to another is an easy process:

1. Click on the Start button and click the arrow next to the **Shut down** button (A in Fig. 5) and click on **Switch user** (B). The screen will then display the account pictures of each user of the computer.

2. The new user should click on their account picture and enter their password (if one has been set).

Note: in order to maintain the security of the computer each user should log off when they have finished working – this prevents unauthorised access of their files by others.

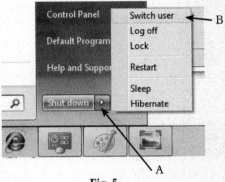

Fig. 5

Section 7:
Creating a Reset Disk

You will need a USB device like a memory stick. CDs cannot be used to create a reset disk. If you have a computer that has a floppy disk drive you can use a blank floppy disk.

1. Click on **Start**, then on **Control Panel**, and in large or small icons view click on **User Accounts**.

2. Click on **Create a password reset disk** (A in Fig. 6) in the task pane.

3. Insert your USB device or floppy disk.

4. The **Forgotten Password Wizard** opens.

5. Follow the Wizard's instructions and enter your current password when prompted. Click the **Next** button (B) to move on to the next set of instructions.

6. When the Wizard has finished, remove your disk or device and store in a safe place. Remember that anyone else can use the reset disk to gain access to your computer.

Fig. 6

Section 8:
Windows 7 – So What's New?

There are many new things to discover with Windows 7. Here are a few:

Getting Started

This is a link on the Start menu. If you click on **Getting Started** while connected to the Internet, Internet Explorer

8 and the Microsoft website for Windows 7 will open. Here you can watch mini videos on how to use the operating system. There are other useful links which you may find interesting to investigate.

Appearance and Aero Features

Windows 7 provides a streamlined environment and an uncluttered interface compared to earlier versions of Windows. There are fewer steps necessary to complete tasks, making the program easier to use and more efficient. The Aero experience now includes the features Aero Snap, Aero Peek and Aero Shake. The Aero Glass feature, available in various colours, gives a transparency to the windows borders and title bars which allows other objects or windows on the desktop to be viewed through them. But to make life even easier Aero Peek means you can see through all parts of all open windows in order to view the desktop – just at the touch of a button. Aero Snap lets you move a program window to the left or right and to maximise and minimise it. By using the mouse cursor to select and 'shake' a title bar, Aero Shake lets you minimise/maximise all the windows open except the one you are viewing.

Free Software with Windows Live Essentials

Some things which were included in XP and Vista editions are now available to be downloaded, free, from the Internet. These include Photo Gallery, Windows Live Mail, Movie Maker, Messenger, Writer and Family Safety.

These programs can be downloaded individually or as a complete package.

Windows Live Mail

Windows Live Mail is not included in the Windows 7 set-up but can be downloaded for free from the Microsoft website. It replaces the previous versions of Windows Mail and Outlook Express. It's a coherent, streamlined and user-friendly email package which now includes Windows Calendar, Newsfeeds and News group links.

Internet Explorer 8

Windows 7 comes with Microsoft's newest browser, Internet Explorer 8, which has many new features to make surfing the Internet quicker, easier and tailored to your own interests. Accelerators, suggested sites and increased security will enhance your web-surfing experience.

Start Menu and Jump Lists

The Start menu still contains all the familiar features but is now more versatile – programs can be pinned and unpinned from the menu, and jump lists make accessing recently opened or used programs and documents quicker and more efficient.

The Taskbar and Thumbnails

The taskbar has been updated: programs can be pinned to the taskbar and are represented by an icon rather than text. Live thumbnails of multiple windows of a program can now be viewed side by side while the **Show Desktop** button, which enables you to quickly view the desktop, has been moved to the extreme right of the notification area.

Libraries

Libraries are a new feature of Windows 7 and enable you to view in one window similar types of folders which might be stored in different parts of your system.

Action Center

The new Action Center contains a security section and a maintenance section. It alerts you to any problems it detects in your computer system and supplies solutions.

Gadgets

The Windows Vista sidebar has gone but the gadgets have become more versatile, and can be placed anywhere you wish on the desktop. More can be downloaded from the Internet.

Entertainment

Windows Media Player and Windows Media Center enable your computer to become a hub for your entertainment needs; you can watch movies, DVDs and TV, play and download music, create and burn CD/DVDs, and much more.

Chapter Two:
Getting to Know Windows 7

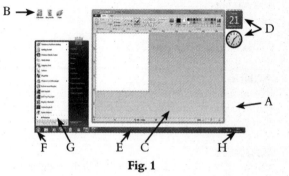

Fig. 1

Section 1:
The Desktop

Once you have installed Windows and set up your user account it's a good idea to familiarise yourself with the desktop and to take time to identify the items described below and shown in Fig. 1.

The **desktop** (A) is the area that you view as your computer opens once you have logged in. It's the area where all the program windows open and where you work. It provides the route to programs, pictures, files and documents that you store on your computer as well as housing shortcuts to programs and handy gadgets.

Icons (B) are shortcuts into programs and files. They can be placed onto the desktop or taskbar to provide quick and easy access; they can also be removed when no longer required. Clicking on an icon opens a program window (C) onto the desktop.

Gadgets (D) are small programs that you may find useful to have displayed on the desktop, such as a clock or a calendar.

The **taskbar** (E) is usually positioned across the bottom of the desktop. It can also be moved to other sides of the desktop.

On the left of the taskbar sits the **Start button** (F). It opens the **Start menu** (G), which gives you access to programs and files on Windows 7.

The **notification area** (H) is on the right of the taskbar. It displays the time, date and various icons.

Extra: the Quick Launch toolbar that was present in the Vista edition of Windows is not included in Windows 7.

Section 2:
The Start Menu

The **Start menu** enables you to access the programs, files and folders stored on your computer. If you are used to the XP editions of Windows you will notice some differences with Windows 7, but once you are familiar with the new layout you will find navigation a lot more streamlined. The Start menu is your route into customising your computer and contains jump lists that allow you to quickly access recently used documents and files.

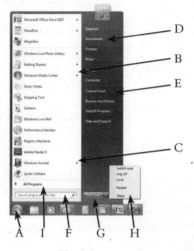

Fig. 2

1. Move your pointer onto the **Start button** (A in Fig. 2) and click once to open the menu. Take time to familiarise yourself with the layout. The programs listed on the left (B) of the Start menu are separated by a horizontal line.
2. Those above the line are **pinned** and remain on the menu – unless you decide to unpin them at a later stage

(see Section 9). The items below the separator line change depending upon those which you most frequently use.

3. A program which has an arrow next to it gives you access through **jump lists** (C) to recently used documents and files (see Section 12).

4. The commands on the right side remain the same. Those at the top of the list are folders – also called **Libraries** (D) – which contain your documents, pictures, music, games and other files (see Chapter Four, Section 1).

5. Below these folders are **command buttons** (E) which give you access to information and programs installed on the computer (see Chapter Three, Section 1).

6. The **instant search box** (F) which is located above the Start button enables you to search both the computer and the Internet (see Chapter Five, Section 2).

7. The **power off** button (G) and **shutdown menu** (H) allow you to turn off the computer or select other options such as logging off, or putting the computer to sleep. **All Programs** (I) expands the Start menu.

Section 3:
All Programs

There are many more programs than can be listed on the first part of the Start menu, which expands to display more.

1. Click on **All Programs** and the Start menu expands to show a list of further programs (A in Fig. 3).

2. To see more programs that are attached to the Start menu use the scroll bar (B) and scroll down the list.

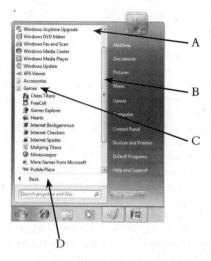

Fig. 3

Some similar types of programs are grouped together in folders (C); for example, the games on Windows 7 are collected together in the Games folder.

3. Click once on the Games folder and the individual programs will be listed. To close the Games folder, click on it once.
4. To get back to the original Start menu click on **Back** (D).
5. To close the Start menu, move the pointer onto a vacant section of the desktop and click once.

Section 4:
The Taskbar

The Windows 7 taskbar looks different to previous taskbars and is certainly more versatile. It includes the **Start button** (A in Fig. 4) of course and also the following elements as shown:

Program and Taskbar buttons

A taskbar button will always appear whenever you have a program open on the desktop. When programs are opened, **shortcut buttons** (B) are displayed on the taskbar. Allow your mouse to hover over a taskbar button and the name of the relevant program appears on a small label (C). Some programs, such as Windows Explorer and Internet Explorer, are pinned by default to the taskbar but you can also choose to pin and unpin other programs to give you quick access to the programs you use most frequently (see Section 8 on how to pin and unpin a program). If you don't like the look of the taskbar it can be personalised (see Chapter Seven, Section 8).

The Show Desktop Button

(See A in Fig. 5.) This is a re-designed feature that minimises all open windows to display the desktop. Click on it once to minimise all programs and then click again to reopen the programs onto the desktop. To view the desktop without minimising programs, allow the mouse cursor to just hover over the button.

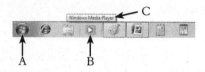

Fig. 4

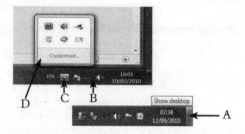

Fig. 5

Fig. 6

The Notification Area

(See B in Fig. 5.) This shows the clock, volume mixer, online connection button, and the hidden icons button. Click on the **Hidden icons** button (C) and a display (D) will show all the icons not currently on view. It's also the place where small pop-up windows called notifications (A in Fig. 6) will appear giving information about progress and status on such things as downloads. (See Chapter Seven, Section 8 for how to customise the notification area.)

Extra: when the computer is put into sleep mode it is placed in a state of very low energy – a good way to save power and help the environment.

Section 5:
The Shut Down Menu

At some point when you have finished working you will need to close down your computer. Other options help you to protect your work from being viewed by other users. This includes logging off, switching user accounts or putting your computer to sleep.

1. Move your pointer onto the **Start menu button** (A in Fig. 7) and click once, then across onto the **Shut down arrow** (B).
2. The menu (C) displays the options available. Move the pointer onto the option you have selected and click once.

Shut down

Choose this option when you want to completely close down the computer and the power supply. Remember to save any work that you have done and to close any open programs.

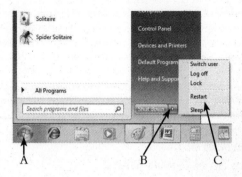

Fig. 7

Switch User

Use to switch between the different users of the computer. Programs that you are currently using do not need to be closed but you will have to enter your password to resume.

Log off

Logging off preserves privacy and protects your account from other users, but you will need to save your work and then close any programs that you are using and then log on again to resume.

Lock

This option prevents others accessing your computer should you leave it unattended. Programs continue to run, so you do not have to save and close your work. To resume you will need to enter your password.

Restart

Using the restart option can help to solve minor problems such as the screen freezing or programs not responding. But any open programs will automatically close and you may lose any work that has not already been saved.

Sleep

Choose this option if you do not share your computer with others but wish to leave it for a while. Windows will automatically save your work. To re-awaken, press the power button. The programs that you are currently using will remain open. This is not password protected and your work can be viewed by anyone 'waking up' the computer.

Section 6:
The Mouse

A mouse can come in a variety of styles and on laptops there's an integral mouse pad. On a conventional mouse the left button is used to move a pointer or cursor on the screen and to click and double-click. The wheel allows you to quickly scroll through pages. The right button opens a drop-down menu. On a laptop, the cursor is worked by moving your finger across the mouse pad and using the two adjacent buttons to left or right-click. Other pointing devices are also available.

Note: when typing text the cursor changes to an I-beam.

Clicking and the Double-click

1. To single click, press the *left* mouse button once.
2. To double-click press the left button twice in rapid succession.
3. If double-clicking is a problem, use a single left-click and then press the Enter key on your keyboard. *Also* read Chapter Seven, Section 10 to see how to slow down the click rate.

Click and Drag

1. Place the pointer over the **Recycle Bin** icon which sits on the desktop.
2. Left-click and hold your finger down.
3. Keeping the button depressed, move the pointer across the screen, and it will drag the icon with it.
4. Release the button and the icon remains in its new position.
5. Return the icon to its original place.

Are you left-handed?

If so, the functions of the mouse buttons can be swapped over. Read Chapter Seven, Section 10 to see how you can customise the mouse.

Practising Mouse Control

The game of Solitaire is ideal for practising mouse control, double-clicking and click-and-drag. To open click on **Start**, then on **All Programs**, **Games** and **Solitaire**. Click once on the deck of cards and the cards will turn over. To move a card from one place to another, use the click-and-drag technique. Double-click on an ace and it will automatically jump into one of the four empty spaces.

Section 7:
The Keyboard

Keyboards vary in style but most are similar in appearance. Fig. 8 shows the main section of the keyboard. Fig. 9 shows the right side of the keyboard with the arrow keys and a numeric pad.

Note the following keys:

Windows key (A in Fig. 8): This displays the Windows logo. Press this key and it will open the Start menu. There are other programs that also use this key as a shortcut.

Tab key (B): This can be used to move between different parts of a dialog box or a window. It is also used to indent text in a word document.

Arrow keys (A in Fig. 9): These four keys, with arrows pointing up, down, left and right, can be used to move the I-beam in a text box or document, and the pointer.

Try this:
1. Press the Windows key (Fig. 10). The Start menu opens.
2. Press the upward-pointing arrow and the highlight moves up the menu.

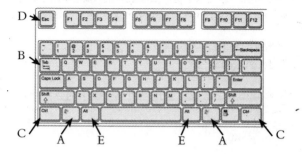

Fig. 8

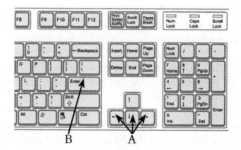

Fig. 9

Fig. 10

3. Press the downward-pointing arrow and the highlight moves down.
4. Press the right-pointing arrow and the highlight moves onto the command buttons.
5. Press the Windows key and the Start menu closes.

Enter key (B in Fig. 9): Press this to start a new line when typing text or to make a selection.

Try this:
1. Press the Windows key.
2. Press the upward-pointing arrow and move the highlight onto **All Programs**.
3. Press the **Enter** key. The expanded list opens.
4. Use the upward-pointing arrow to move through the list. Select a program by pressing **Enter** and the program window opens.
5. Close the program by left-clicking with the mouse on the red cross in the top right corner of the window.

Control Keys
These can be used alone or combined with other keys to perform certain actions. **Try this:**
1. Press Ctrl (C in Fig. 8) and hold the key down. Press Esc (D) and then release both keys.
2. The Start menu opens and remains on the screen.
3. Click anywhere on the screen to close the menu.

*Extra: there are many more keyboard moves. Open Help and Support (see Chapter Five) and type **using the keyboard** into the Search box to discover more.*

Section 8:
Programs

A program can be opened from the Start menu, taskbar or an icon that has been created and placed on the desktop.

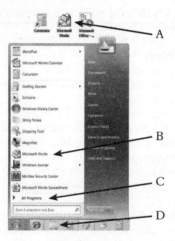

Fig. 11

Open from a Desktop Icon

1. Place the pointer onto the desktop icon for the program you wish to open, for example Microsoft Works (A in Fig. 11).

2. Double-click on the icon or click once and press Enter on the keyboard, and the program will open.

Open from the Start Menu

1. Click on **Start**.
2. Look on the **Start menu** (B in Fig. 11) for the program you wish to use.
3. If it is not listed, click on **All Programs** to view more (C).
4. Locate the program, click on it and the program window will open.

Open from the Taskbar

Some program icons appear on the taskbar by default.
1. Place the pointer on the program icon (D).
2. Click once and the program window will open on the desktop.

Close a Program Window

1. Click on the **Close** button or
2. Right-click on the title bar at the top of the window and click on **Close** on the drop-down menu.

*Extra: to quickly find a program, type its name into the **Start Search** box at the bottom of the **Start menu**. If it has been installed on your computer, it will then appear in the Start menu. See more about searching in Chapter Five.*

Section 9:
Pinning a Program

Pinning a program is a unique feature of Windows 7. A program icon can be pinned to the Start menu or to the taskbar. It will remain displayed until you decide you wish

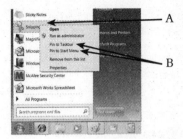

Fig. 12

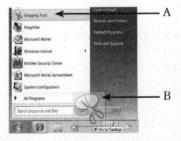

Fig. 13

Fig. 14

to unpin it. This allows you quick access to a program that you frequently use.

Pin a Program to the Start Menu or Taskbar

1. Click on the Start button and locate the program you wish to pin.
2. Right-click on the program and a list (A in Fig. 12) is displayed.
3. Click **Pin to Start Menu** or click **Pin to Taskbar** (B).
4. *Or* right-click on the program icon (A in Fig. 13) on the Start menu and holding the mouse button down, drag the icon (B) onto the taskbar, and release the button.

Pin an Open Program to the Taskbar

1. Right-click the taskbar button of an open program.
2. Click on **Pin this program to taskbar**.

Unpin a Program from the Start Menu

If you no longer wish to keep a program pinned it can be easily removed.
1. Click on the Start button and locate the program you wish to unpin.
2. Right-click on the program.
3. Click **Remove from this list**.

Unpin a Program from the Taskbar

1. Right-click the taskbar button of a pinned program.
2. Click on **Unpin this program from taskbar** (A in Fig. 14).

*Extra: to remove an icon from the Desktop right-click it and then click **Delete** on the drop-down menu. Click **Yes** to confirm. The icon is sent to the Recycle Bin.*

Section 10:
Windows

A window allows you to view the contents of a program; you can have more than one window or program open at a time. The window is defined by the **window border** (A in Fig. 15). Across the top of a window is the **title bar** (B). In the top right hand corner are the **sizing buttons** (C) which allow you to alter the size and position of a window.

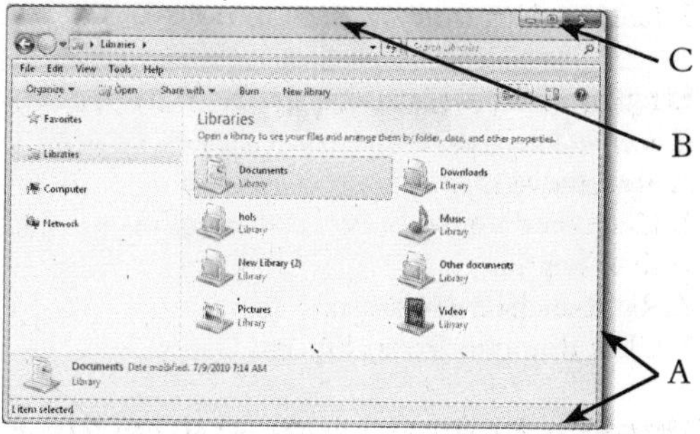

Fig. 15

Using the Window Sizing Buttons
Minimize
1. Click on the **Minimize** button (A in Fig. 16). The window shrinks to become a button on the taskbar.
2. Click on the taskbar button and the window reopens on the desktop.

Maximize
1. Click on **Maximize** (B in Fig. 16). The window expands to fill the whole screen. It loses its borders and cannot be moved or resized. The central button changes to **Restore Down** (A in Fig. 17).
2. Click on **Restore Down** and the window will return to its original size.
Resizing a window
A window can be resized horizontally, vertically or diagonally.
1. Move the pointer to any edge or corner of the window's border; the pointer changes to a double-headed arrow.
2. Left-click and, keeping the button depressed, drag the pointer to reduce or increase the size of the window. Release the button.

Close a Window
Close the window by clicking on **Close** (B in Fig. 17).

Moving a Window Using the Title Bar
You cannot move a maximised window using the title bar, so click the restore down button first.

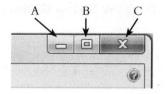

Fig. 16

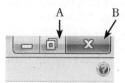

Fig. 17

1. Move the pointer onto the title bar (B in Fig. 15), left-click, hold down the button and drag the window to its new position.
2. Release the button.

Section 11:
Gadgets

Gadgets are small programs that can sit anywhere you wish on the desktop. They may be things that you find useful or fun, such as local weather information, clock, calendar, picture puzzles or slide shows.

Place a Gadget on the Desktop

1. Right-click any empty section of the desktop and from the menu (A in Fig. 18) click on **Gadgets**.
2. Choose a gadget from the gallery (A in Fig. 19) and double-click the one you want, or you can *left-click* the gadget and drag it onto the desktop, or you can *right-click* the gadget and click on **Add** from the menu (B).
3. The gadget (C) appears on your desktop.

Move a Gadget

1. Use the **gadget buttons** to move a gadget to any desktop position.
2. Move the pointer onto a gadget and the gadget buttons appear.
3. Left-click on the dot grid or **Drag gadget button** (A in Fig. 20) and holding the mouse button down drag the gadget to its new position on the screen and release the button.

Close a Gadget

1. Move the pointer onto the gadget and the gadget buttons appear.
2. Click on **Close gadget** (B).

Change the size of a Gadget

1. Move the pointer onto the gadget and if the gadget can be resized a toggle button will appear (A in Fig. 21).
2. Click on the toggle and the gadget will either get larger or smaller.

Fig. 18

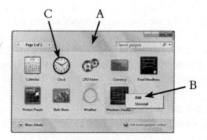

Fig. 19

Fig. 20

Changing a Gadget using the Options Button

Most gadgets can be personalised. For example, you can change the style of the clock, choose a different puzzle or alter the pictures in the slide show.

1. Move the pointer onto a gadget so that the gadget buttons appear.
2. Click on the **gadget options** button (B).
3. Select your options and then click OK.

Get More Information from a Gadget

Some gadgets also give you direct access to information online. For example, the weather gadget allows you to choose from areas around the globe (A in Fig. 22) and then gives you a direct web link to MSN weather (C in Fig. 21).

The newsfeed gadget gives you access to current news stories. You can select which area the feeds come from, read a brief synopsis of the story or click the link to read more.

Get More Gadgets

More gadgets can be obtained online.

1. Open the gadgets gallery.
2. Click on the link **Get more gadgets online**.

Extra: only download gadgets from reputable sites. Suspect sites could use a gadget to transfer a Trojan virus or other malware onto your computer (see Chapter Ten for more on making your computer secure).

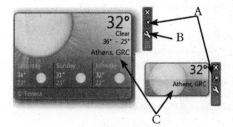

Fig. 21

Fig. 22

Section 12:
Jump Lists

Jump lists are a new feature of Windows 7 – they are designed to save you time and to lead you quickly into recently opened documents, to tasks and functions within a program, or straight into the program itself. A small arrow pointing to the right of a program name in the Start menu shows that a jump list is available. Jump lists can also be accessed from the taskbar.

Jump Lists on the Start Menu
1. Click on the **Start** button.
2. Rest your pointer on **Getting Started** (A in Fig. 23) to see the jump list of tasks (B). Click on an item to open.
3. On the right pane of the Start menu, rest your pointer on **Recent Items**. This jump list will show the names of those items that you have been working on most recently.

Note: in Windows 7, Recent Items is not present by default on the Start menu, but it can be added. See Chapter Seven, Section 9 for details on how.

Jump Lists on the Taskbar
1. Right-click a program (A in Fig. 24) on the taskbar.
2. Left-click on the item you wish to open (B).

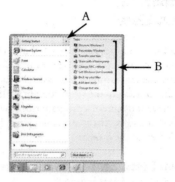

Fig. 23

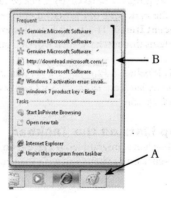

Fig. 24

Section 13:
'Getting Started' and Windows Live Essentials

1. Make sure you are connected to the Internet then click on the **Start** button, and move your pointer onto **Getting Started**.

2. From the jump list click on **Discover Windows 7** to open Microsoft's website dedicated to Windows 7.

3. There are some useful videos (A in Fig. 25) on getting started – click on the play button to start the video.

4. Scroll (B) further down the page to a number of tabs with helpful guides to lead you gently through some aspects of Windows 7.

Free Software to Download

As an owner of a genuine edition of Microsoft Windows 7 you are entitled to free software including the email package Windows Live Mail, Movie Maker, Photo Gallery, Messenger and Family Safety.

1. Click on the **Start** button, rest your pointer on **Getting Started** and click on **Get Windows Live Essentials** on the jump list.

2. Make sure you are connected to the Internet and then click on **Discover Windows 7**.

3. You can download the Live Essentials as a complete package or, if you prefer, the individual components can be downloaded as and when you are ready to explore and use them.

Fig. 25

Fig. 26

Chapter Three:
Working with Windows

Section 1:
The Basic Layout

One of the advantages of using Explorer windows is that they all have the same consistent layout. Get to know the organisation of one Explorer window and you will be able to successfully navigate the others.

1. Click the **Start** button.
2. Click on **Pictures** and the Pictures Explorer window opens.

See Fig. 1 for the items described below. Remember: this is just representative of other Explorer windows.

The Command Bar (A)
This shows the various commands for working within a particular window. The Command Buttons vary, with individual windows carrying command buttons that are relevant to the subject. All windows show **Organize** (B).

Back/Forward buttons (C)
These will take you back and forth between previously viewed windows; click on the adjacent down arrow (G) to see a list of previous windows you have visited.

C G B   E A   D F

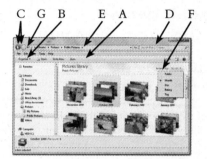

Fig. 1

A

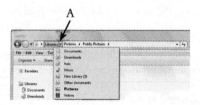

Fig. 2

Search: (D)

Type in a query and then click on the magnifying glass and
Windows 7 will search for the required item.

The Address Bar (E)

Use the address bar to return to previous locations. Click
on a black arrow for a list of previously visited windows
(see also A in Fig. 2).

Arrange by: (F)

This drop-down list enables you to view the windows folders arranged by Month, Day, Rating or Tag.

The Menu Bar

This contains a row of buttons which are used less frequently but which you may need to access from time to time. The menu bar is not shown by default but as it is very useful it's worthwhile choosing to enable its display.

Enable Menu Bar

Click on **Organize** (A in Fig. 3), **Layout** (B) and finally on **Menu Bar** (C). The menu bar will then appear above the command bar.

Section 2:
The Panes of a Window

A window is divided up into sections called panes. These panes allow you to access libraries, files and folders and to navigate between them. You might find it useful to have all the panes open initially so that you can see what each one offers and then close those you do not require.

Viewing the Window Explorer panes

1. Click on **Organize** (A in Fig. 3) and a drop-down menu appears.
2. Select **Layout** (B), click whichever panes you want to include. A tick will appear alongside the selected pane name.

Note: to hide a pane, click to remove the tick.

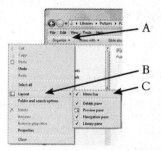

Fig. 3

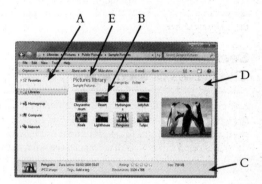

Fig. 4

Navigation Pane

(See A in Fig. 4) This is the pane on the far left where the various categories of common folders are displayed: Favorites, Libraries, Homegroup, Computer and Network.

Contents Pane (B)

Click on a folder in the navigation pane and its contents are displayed in the next pane to the right: contents pane.

Details Pane (C)

Click on a file or folder in the contents pane and further information about it will be displayed in the details pane, which runs along the bottom.

The Preview Pane (D)

The preview pane (to the right of the contents pane) allows you to quickly preview a file without having to open files individually. Simply click once on a file in the contents pane to see it displayed in the preview pane.

Library Pane (E)

This sits at the top of the contents pane and enables you to navigate folders contained within the various libraries.

Section 3:
Window Thumbnails

One of the really useful things about Windows 7 is that you can have more than one window or program open at once. So you could, for example, have several word document windows open at the same time as some web page windows. When these windows are minimised Windows 7 will organise them efficiently into groups under a program button on the taskbar (A in Fig. 5) – this helps to keep the desktop orderly.

B

A

Fig. 5

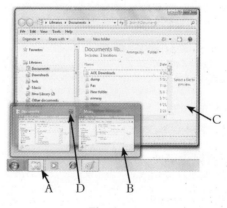

C

A D B

Fig. 6

When a program window is open it can be minimised onto a button on the taskbar. To check the name and content of the window move the pointer onto the program icon on the taskbar, allow it to hover and a thumbnail of the program window appears (B).

Open a New Program Window

If you already have a program window open, you can open a further window in the same program by *right-clicking* on the program taskbar button. Click on the program name and a new window opens.

Switching Windows Using Thumbnails

If you have more than one window open in a program, thumbnails can be used to switch between windows.

1. Hover the pointer over the program icon (A in Fig. 6) and the windows currently open within that program are displayed as thumbnails (B).

2. Move the pointer onto a thumbnail and the full size version appears on the desktop (C).

3. To make a window active click on the relevant thumbnail and it will open on the desktop and the other thumbnails will close.

4. You can chose to close a window by clicking on the **Close** button of a thumbnail (D).

Section 4:
Switching Windows Using
Windows flip

Windows flip is a speedy way of 'flipping' through open windows which have been minimised; it allows you to find the one you want and then make it active.

Fig. 7

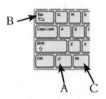

Fig. 8

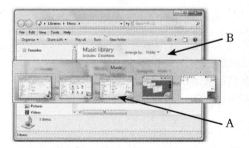

Fig. 9

1. Locate the **Windows** and **Tab** keys (A and B in Fig. 8). First, press the Windows key and then the Tab key.
2. The programs that you are currently running will appear across the screen as overlapping windows (as shown in Fig. 7).
3. To slow the rate of flipping, continue to press the Windows key and depress and release the Tab key until you have found the one you want to view at the front of the stack.
4. Stop pressing the keys and the window you have chosen becomes active.

Switching Windows by Cycling Through Thumbnails

Windows 7 allows you to cycle through the thumbnails (e.g. A in Fig. 9) of any program windows that you have running and then to open the one that you wish to be active (B). This only works when you have open program windows minimised on the taskbar.

1. Locate the **Alt** and **Tab** keys (C and B in Fig. 8).
2. Press the Alt key and then press and release the Tab key so that each of the program thumbnails is highlighted in turn.
3. Each window appears behind the thumbnails. When you locate the window that you wish to view, release the keys and the program window you have selected stays open on the desktop.

Note: if you keep your finger depressed on the Tab key the highlight will move too rapidly through the thumbnails. By releasing and then pressing the Tab you will have time to view and select a window.

Section 5:
Using Aero Snap to Move and Change the Size of a Window

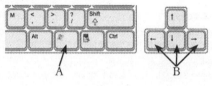

Fig. 10

Aero Snap is a feature that allows you to maximise, minimise or move a window using the **Windows key** and the **arrow keys** on the keyboard (A and B in Fig. 10).

Moving a Window to the Left or Right

1. Open a program so that the window is displayed on the desktop.
2. Press the Windows key and the left arrow and the open window moves to the left.
3. To move the open window to the right, press the Windows key and right arrow key.

Maximise and Minimise a Window

1. Open a program so that the window is displayed on the desktop.
2. To maximise the open window, press the Windows key and the up arrow.
3. To restore down, press the Windows key and the down arrow.

4. To minimise from restore down, press the Windows key and the down arrow.

5. Left-click with the mouse to reopen from the taskbar button.

Section 6:
Aero Shake

Minimise all Open Windows

If you have a number of windows open and wish to minimise all except one, you can use Aero Shake.

1. Place your pointer (B in Fig. 11) on the title bar (A) of the window you wish to keep open.

2. Depress the left mouse button and drag the title bar back and forth as if shaking it.

3. All the other open windows will minimise onto the taskbar.

4. To restore the other windows, 'shake' the active window title bar again.

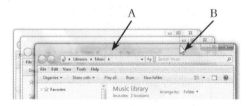

Fig. 11

Section 7:
More Ways to View and Change the Size of a Window

Cascade, Stack or Show Windows Side by Side

1. Right-click on the taskbar (A in Fig 12).
2. Click on **Cascade**, **Show window stacked** or **Show windows side by side** (B).
3. Any open windows will be rearranged on the screen depending upon which option you have chosen.
4. To undo the arrangement, right-click again on the taskbar. Left-click **Undo**.

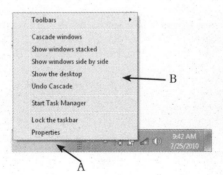

Fig. 12

Using the Window Sizing Menu

This menu lists the functions of the sizing buttons and is an alternative way to resize a window.

1. Click on the icon in the very top left corner of the window to open the sizing menu (A in Fig. 13).
2. Select an action from the menu (B).

Section 8:
Aero Peek and the Desktop

Aero peek is a quick way to look at the desktop without having to go to the trouble of closing or minimising any program windows.

1. Locate the **Show desktop** button (A in Fig. 14) and allow the pointer to hover over the button.
2. Any open windows will disappear and be represented by black outlines (B). The desktop below will be visible so that gadgets (C) and icons (D) are displayed.
3. Remove the pointer from the button and the open windows reappear.

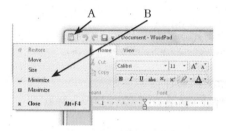

Fig. 13

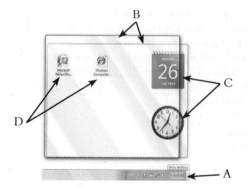

Fig. 14

Chapter Four:
Working with Libraries, Folders and Files

Libraries are a new feature of Windows 7. Four are included by default: Documents, Pictures, Music and Videos. The library and folder structure enables you to group together folders and files from various locations, in the way that best suits you. You can also create your own new Libraries.

Section 1:
Accessing Libraries

Open a Library from the Taskbar or Start Menu

1. Click the **Windows Explorer** button on the taskbar (H in Fig. 1) or click on one of the library buttons on the right pane of the Start menu.
2. Windows Explorer opens on the desktop showing the various Libraries in the contents pane (D).
3. Double-click on a library to view its folders in the contents pane.

(For more on how to display panes, see Chapter Three, Section 2.)

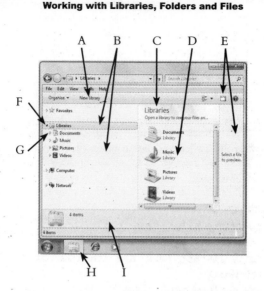

Fig. 1

Open a Library or Folder from the Navigation Pane

1. Click the *open triangle* by **Library** (G) in the navigation pane and a list of the individual libraries it holds (B) are listed in the navigation pane.

2. Click an *open triangle* by the side of a library, such as Documents, and the various folders it holds are also listed in the navigation pane.

3. A triangle of any sort next to a library shows that it contains further libraries or folders.

4. A **black solid** triangle (F in Fig. 1) alongside a library indicates that it is opened; a closed library will have an **open** triangle by its side.

5. Click on the name of a folder in the navigation pane and the files it contains are shown in the contents pane.

The Library, Details and Preview Panes

1. The Library pane (C in Fig. 1) enables you to view the locations of your folders and to also arrange a library's contents in various ways. This pane sits across the top of the contents pane.

2. The Details pane (I) sits across the bottom on the window and gives details of a file.

3. Click on an individual file in the contents pane and it is previewed in the preview pane (E).

4. The **New library** button (A in Fig. 1) sits on the command bar.

Section 2:
Creating a New Library

As in previous editions of Windows, there is more than just one way of doing things. Here are two ways of creating a new library – use whichever one you prefer.

Create and Name a New Library in the Contents Pane

1. Click the Windows Explorer button on the taskbar and click on **Libraries** (A in Fig. 2) in the navigation pane.

2. Click on the **New library** button (B) on the toolbar and a new library is displayed in the contents pane.

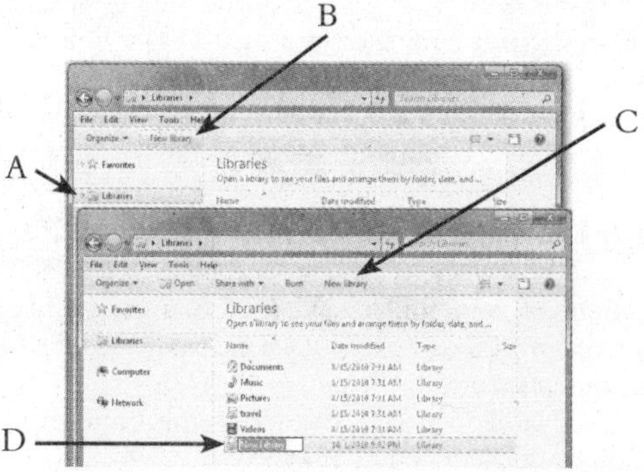

Fig. 2

3. Click in the text box (D) and type in a name.
4. Click on a clear part of the contents pane and the name is saved (or press Enter on the keyboard).
5. To add another new library click on the New library (C) button.

Create and Name a New Library in the Navigation Pane

1. Click the Windows Explorer button on the taskbar.
2. In the navigation pane right-click on **Libraries** and a drop-down list displays.
3. Click on **New** and then **Library** and a new library is created in the *navigation pane*.
4. Left-click in the text box and type in a name for the new library.

Section 3:
Organising a Library

1. In the navigation pane, click on a library.
2. In the Library pane, click on the down arrow by **Folder** (A in Fig. 3).
3. The drop-down list offers different ways of arranging the contents.
4. Click on **Folder** to show the folders and separate files.
5. The options shown below Folder (B) allow you to arrange the library files in whichever manner you choose. These options vary between the Music, Documents, Pictures and Video libraries.

Include a Folder in a New Library that you have Created

1. Click your new library (A in Fig. 4) in the navigation pane.
2. Click on **Include a folder** (B) in the contents pane.
3. Navigate to the folder (C) that you wish to add to the Library.
4. Click on it and then on **Include folder** (D) and the folder is added to the new library.

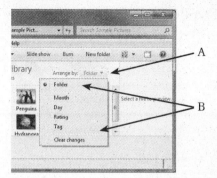

Fig. 3

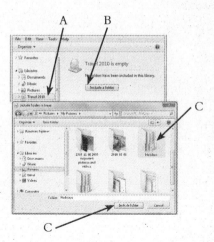

Fig. 4

Add a Folder to a Current Library

1. Open Windows Explorer and in the navigation pane locate the folder that you wish to add to a library.
2. Right-click the folder (A in Fig. 5) and from the drop-down menu, select **Open folder location** (B).
3. The folder will appear in the contents pane.
4. Click on the **Include in library** (C) button on the toolbar and from the drop-down menu click on the library you have chosen for the folder destination.

Rename a Library

1. Click on **Libraries** in the navigation pane.
2. Right-click an individual library, and from the drop-down menu click on **Rename**.
3. Press delete to remove the existing name and then type in the new name and press Enter to save.

Remove a Folder from a Library

1. In the navigation pane, click on the library (A in Fig. 6) which holds the folder you wish to remove.
2. In the libraries pane, click on the **Locations** link (B).
3. A dialog box displays the folders contained in the library.
4. Click on the folder you wish to remove (C) and then click the **Remove** button (D) and click **OK** (E).

Note: you will not have deleted the folder, simply removed it from the library. The folder will remain stored in its original location.

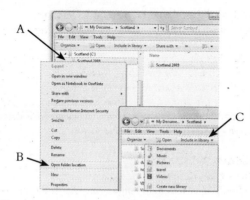

Fig. 5

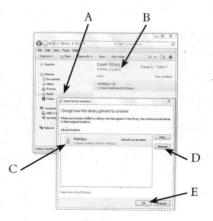

Fig. 6

Section 4:
Accessing Folders and Files

Folders can contain single files and other folders. The **folders list** is located in the navigation pane and enables you to access your libraries, folders and files. Just like with Libraries, a *black solid triangle* (A in Fig. 7) alongside a folder indicates that it is opened; a closed folder will have an *open triangle* (B) by its side. If a folder has no triangle by its side then it doesn't contain any folders but it may contain files.

Open and Close a Folder

1. Click on any folder in the folders list and you will notice that its triangle changes from an open triangle to a solid one.
2. Further folders contained within the one that you clicked open will be listed below and also shown in the contents pane.
3. Close a folder by clicking on its solid triangle.

Open a File

Files that are contained in a library or folder can be opened from the contents pane. In Fig. 7 the Pictures library is used as an example.
1. Click on **Libraries** (C) in the navigation pane.
2. Double-click on the **Pictures library** in the contents pane.
3. Double-click on the **Sample Pictures** folder and the individual files are displayed in the contents pane (D).
4. Double-click on a file (E) and it will open fully onto the screen in the appropriate program.

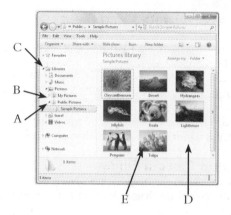

Fig. 7

Close a File

Click on the **Close** button in the top right-hand corner of the window.

Section 5:
Viewing Your Files and Folders in the Contents Pane

The options button on the command bar gives you a choice of how to view your files and folders in the contents pane

(A in Fig. 8). The pictures in Fig. 8 are arranged by month – click on **Arrange by** (B) to organise files differently.

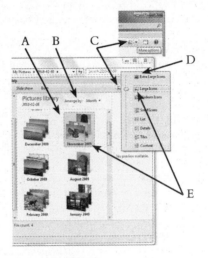

Fig. 8

Choosing a View

1. To choose a view click on the **Options** button (C).
2. The options drop-down list opens (D).
3. The view selected in Fig. 8 is of **Large Icons** (E).

There are four main ways of viewing files and folders: Icons, Details, Tiles and List. The different views are useful for different types of files. You may find it more useful, for example, to view picture files in Extra Large Icons view, which would enable you to view the visual details of the photos more easily. If you want to see information about the size of a Word document, for example, and the date it was created, then you would choose Details view.

Icons View

Choose from Small, Medium, Large and Extra Large. With Extra Large there's no file preview available in the preview pane.

Details View

This view lists files and folders along with details of date modified, type, size and tags.

Tiles View

This shows an icon with the name of the file or folder along with its type.

List View

This is a simple list of files and folders. There may be more than one column if there are a lot of items. Use the horizontal scroll bar to view other columns.

*Extra: click on the **View** button on the menu bar and the drop-down menu also lists the different file viewing options – click to select.*

Section 6:
Creating and Naming Folders

As you create more files you will need to organise them into folders and give them meaningful names in order to identify them. At some point you may also wish to change the name of a file or folder.

Create and Name a New Folder

There are a number of ways to create a new folder. This is one of the quickest.

1. Click on a library or folder (A in Fig. 9) in the navigation pane.

2. Make sure you have selected **Folder** (B) from the **Arrange by** options menu.

3. Click on **New folder** (C) on the command bar and the new folder appears in the contents pane.

4. Press delete on the keyboard to remove the words **New folder** (D) and type in a name.

5. Click on a blank section of the contents pane (E) or press **Enter** to save the name.

Here are some other ways to create a new folder using the mouse right-click:

1. Click on a folder in the navigation pane, right-click on the contents pane, click **New,** then **Folder**. The new folder appears in the contents pane.

2. In the navigation pane, right-click on the name of the library or the folder (B in Fig. 10) that will hold the new folder. From the drop-down menu click on **New** (C), then **Folder** (D) and the new folder appears in the navigation pane.

Renaming a File or Folder

1. In the contents pane locate the folder or file to be renamed and click on it.

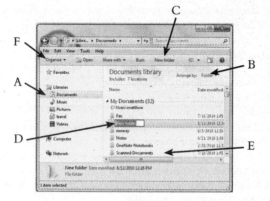

Fig. 9

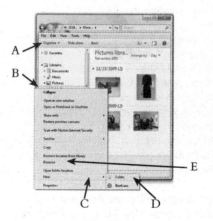

Fig. 10

2. Click on **Organize** (A in Fig. 10) on the command bar. Click on **Rename** (E) on the drop-down menu.

3. The folder or file to be renamed is highlighted.

4. Delete the old name. Type in the new name.

5. Press **Enter** or click on a blank section of the contents pane to save.

*Another way to rename: click on the file or folder to be renamed and right-click the mouse and then, click **Rename** on the drop-down menu.*

Undoing a Rename

1. Click on **Edit** on the menu bar (if not already open, click on Organize, Layout, Menu bar) and click on **Undo Rename**.

2. The original name will be restored.

Renaming a Group of Files

1. Highlight the files or folders you wish to rename by clicking the left mouse button and keeping it depressed as you drag the pointer across them, then release the button (see A in Fig. 11). It's easier to highlight groups of files in List or Details view. Click on the down arrow for viewing options (B).

2. Click on **Organize** (C). From the drop-down menu, click on **Rename** (D). Type in a new name.

3. Press **Enter** or click on a blank section of the contents pane and the new name will be saved. Each file or folder in the group will carry the new name and be numbered consecutively.

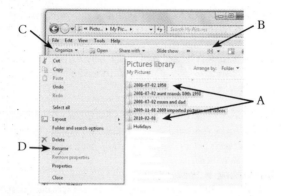

Fig. 11

Section 7:
Copying and Moving Files or Folders

The Explorer windows make it easy to make a copy of a file or a folder. There are several ways to make a copy: using the Edit on the menu bar or the right-click of the mouse button. You may already have a preference for one particular method but it's useful to know the others too.

Using Edit on the Menu Bar to Copy a File or Folder

1 In the contents pane select the file or folder (A in Fig. 12) that you wish to copy.

2. Click on **Edit** (B) on the menu bar and click on **Copy to folder** (C) on the drop-down menu.

3. In the dialog box click on the destination folder (D) for the copied file or folder.

4. Click on the **Copy** (E) button and the item will be copied into the new location.

A quicker way is to use the Edit menu and bypass the dialog box:

1. In the contents pane select the file or folder that you wish to copy.

2. Click **Edit** on the menu bar and click **Copy** on the drop-down menu.

3. Click on the new location for the file or folder.

4. Click on **Edit** and on the drop-down menu click on **Paste**.

Copy and Paste Using right-click of the Mouse

1. In the contents pane locate the file or folder that you wish to copy and right-click. On the drop-down menu click **Copy**.

2. Select the destination folder and right-click.

3. From the drop-down menu click on **Paste**.

4. The file has now been copied into the selected folder.

Moving Files or Folders using 'Drag and Drop'

Rather than make a copy of a file or folder you may just wish to move them to a different location. This can be done by using 'drag and drop'.

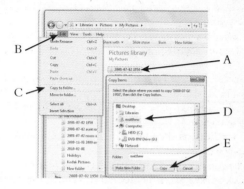

Fig. 12

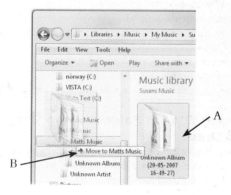

Fig. 13

1. In the contents pane locate the file or folder to be moved (see A in Fig. 13).
2. Click on it, hold down the left mouse button, drag the file into position over the new folder.
3. As the pointer and file icon move over the destination folder a horizontal arrow appears with the folder's name (B). Check that it is the name of the folder you wish to move your file to and release the left mouse button.
4. The file will be dropped into the folder.

Note: click on the folder that has just received the file to check the move has been successful. If you lose your file while moving it, click on **Organize** *and* **Undo**. *The file will be returned to its original folder.*

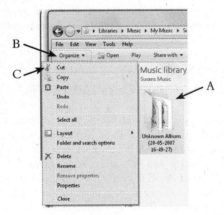

Fig. 14

Moving Files or Folders using Cut and Paste

1. In the contents pane, select the file or folder to be moved (A in Fig. 14).
2. Click on **Organize** (B) on the command bar and click on **Cut** (C) on the drop-down menu. The item fades but does not disappear from the current folder.
3. Click on the new location for the file or folder.
4. Click on **Organize** and on the drop-down menu click on **Paste** and the item is pasted into the new location.

Extra: other ways to Cut and Paste a File or Folder:
*1. Follow the same procedure above but click on **Edit** on the menu bar instead of on Organize.*
*2. In the contents pane locate the file or folder that you wish to move and right-click the mouse button, then on the drop-down menu click **Cut**, select the destination folder and right-click and then click on **Paste**.*

Section 8:
Adding Basic Details to a File

When you save a file, Windows automatically saves certain information with it, such as date created, title, authors, comments and size. You can also add extra details or tags which will help you sort or organise your files. The sort of detail that you can add to a file varies; for example, you can give your photos a star rating, include the author of a Word document or add the name of a music album.

1. Make sure you have the Details pane (A in Fig. 15) open. (Click **Organize** (B), **Layout,** select **Details pane**).
2. Click once on the relevant file (C).
3. The details pane displays the various fields (D) where you enter your information. Click on a field (E) and type your information in the text box that appears.
4. Click on **Save** (F) and the information is added to the file.

Note: to view the information you have added you will need to have the details pane open.

Adding Even More Details to a File

If you wish to change details or add extra tags to a file you can do so by using the **Properties** dialog box.
1. Locate the file concerned in the contents pane.
2. Right-click the file and from the drop-down menu select **Properties**.
3. Click on the **Details** tab and then click on the field concerned to make alterations or additions.
4. Click on **Apply** to save.

Section 9:
Sorting Files and Folders

Files or folders can be sorted into order by fields such as Name, Date tags, Size, Ratings and many more. It is also possible to arrange your files further into groups, which can also be sorted by field. As an example we have used the sample pictures which come with Windows 7, but the same procedure can be used with all the Explorer windows.

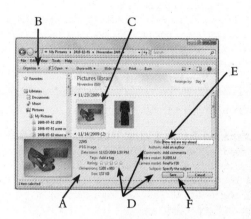

Fig. 15

1. Open the **Pictures library** (A in Fig. 16) in the navigation pane and then in the contents pane double-click on the **Sample Pictures** folder.
2. Right-click on a white section of the contents pane.
3 On the drop-down menu move your pointer onto **Sort by** (B) and a list of fields (C) displays.
4. Click on the field you wish to use to sort your files.

Sorting by Name, Date or Stars

1. Click on **View** (A in Fig. 17) on the menu bar and click on **Details** from the drop-down list. The contents pane is divided into columns, each with a name or header.

2. Each column can sort files using specific filters: e.g. the date column filter uses a range of dates and the rating column uses the number of stars.

3. Move your pointer onto a column header – we have chosen **Name** – and then onto the downward pointing arrow (B) that appears.

4. Click on the arrow.

5. Select the check boxes (C) that you wish to use to filter your files into alphabetical groups.

Note: to reverse the order of any of the columns just click on the column header.

Section 10:
Create a Desktop Shortcut to a File or Folder

A desktop shortcut to a frequently used folder or file is a time saver.

1. Click a file or folder.

2. Click on **File** on the menu bar and on the drop-down menu click on **Create shortcut**.

3. A shortcut will appear on the contents pane. Left-click and drag the shortcut onto the desktop. Release the button.

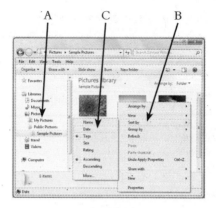

Fig. 16

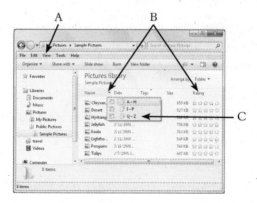

Fig. 17

Extra: you can also create a shortcut by clicking on the file or folder and then right-clicking the mouse button and choosing **Create Shortcut** *from the drop-down menu.*

Section 11: Compressed Files

The amount of room that files and folders take up on your computer can be reduced by compressing them. It's also much faster to send a large file as an email attachment if it has been compressed.

Compressing a File or Folder

1. In the contents pane, select the file or folder (A in Fig. 18) that you want to compress and right-click.
2. Click on **Send to** (B) on the drop-down menu and then on **Compressed (zipped) folder** (C).
3. The newly compressed folder appears, in the contents pane, closed with a zip.
4. Use the same method to compress a folder in the navigation pane. Once compressed it will be shown, closed with a zip, in the navigation pane.

Viewing Compressed Files and Folders

1. Locate the compressed file in the navigation pane and then double-click the file in the contents pane to list its contents.
2. Double-click on a file to open in the appropriate program.

Fig. 18

Uncompress All the Contents of a Compressed File

1. Select the compressed folder (A in Fig. 19) you wish to open and right-click it.

2. On the command bar click on **Extract all files** (B). The **Extract Compressed (Zipped) Folders** wizard opens.

3. A location is pre-selected for the extracted files. To chose a different destination click on **Browse** (C). Select the folder destination for the extracted file (D), then click on **OK** (E). Click, to select the check box by **Show extracted files when complete** (F).

4. Click the **Extract** button (G) and the extracted files will be displayed in your chosen location.

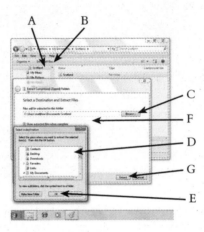

Fig. 19

Viewing and Uncompressing Individual Files and Folders

1. Locate the compressed file in the navigation pane.

2. To just view the file, double-click it in the contents pane and it will open in the relevant program.

3. To uncompress, left-click on the file or folder in the contents pane, drag it across into the navigation pane and drop it into a folder that hasn't been compressed.

4. Click on your chosen destination folder in the navigation pane and the uncompressed file or folder will be listed in the contents pane, available to be opened and worked with.

D   B E   C   A

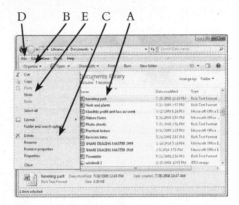

Fig. 20

Section 12:
Deleting Files and Folders

It's a good idea to remove obsolete files or folders on a regular basis as they can take up valuable space on your computer's hard drive.

1. In the contents pane, highlight the file or folder (A in Fig. 20) to be deleted.
2. Click on **Organize** (B) on the command bar. Click on **Delete** (C) from the drop-down menu.
3. A **Delete Folder** or **Delete File** message box is displayed.
4. Click on **Yes** to send the file or folder to the Recycle Bin, click **No** if you have changed your mind.

Extra: other ways to delete a file or folder once you have highlighted the item in the contents pane:
*1. Click on **File** (D) on the menu bar, click **Delete**, click **Yes**.*
*2. Right-click the item, click **Delete**, click **Yes**.*

Undoing a Deletion

If you accidently delete an item you wish to retain, its very easy to get it back by going onto **Organize** and clicking on **Undo** (E) or by right-clicking a blank section of the contents pane and then clicking on **Undo Delete**. In both cases the item will be returned to its original location.

Fig. 21

Open the Recycle Bin

1. Double-click on the Recycle Bin icon (Fig. 21) on the desktop to view its contents.
2. Any deleted files will be listed here.

C   B   A

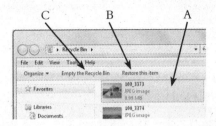

Fig. 22

Restoring a File or Folder

1. Highlight the relevant folder or file (A in Fig. 22) by clicking on it once.
2. Click on **Restore this item** (B) on the command bar.
3. The file will be returned to its original location.

Emptying the Recycle Bin

Eventually you will need to empty the Recycle Bin of unwanted material. If you are confident that you wish to remove all the items in the bin then you can get rid of them all in one go.

1. Click on **Empty the Recycle Bin** (C in Fig. 22) on the command bar.
2. The message box **Delete Multiple Items** will ask you if you are sure that you want to permanently delete all the items.
3. Make your decision and then click on **Yes** or **No**.

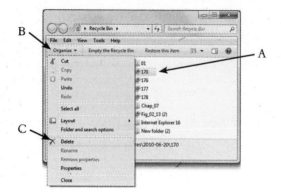

Fig. 23

Deleting a Single Item from the Recycle Bin

1. Left-click the item to be deleted (A in Fig. 23).
2. Click on **Organize** on the command bar (B).
3. Click on **Delete** (C).
4. Confirm deletion by clicking on **Yes** in the message box.

Note: be careful! Once a file, folder or group of items has been deleted from the Recycle Bin it <u>cannot be retrieved</u>. It has been removed forever!

Section 13:
Using a CD or DVD

In order to copy files to a CD or DVD your computer must have a CD/DVD recorder (or burner). Up-to-date computers come with them already installed, but if not, separate recorders can be attached. You can copy word documents, picture files, music and other media onto a CD/DVD; it's a good way of ensuring extra back-up for your files and storing them in a safe environment. Discs can be preformatted to save time later when you copy data onto them. Choose discs that are rewritable (CD-RW and DVD- RW) as you can reuse these many times by erasing from them files that you no longer need. Writable discs (CD-R or DVD-R) can not be erased.

Note: a CD will work in a CD or DVD drive but a DVD will only work in a DVD drive.

Formatting a CD or DVD

1. Insert a writable CD or DVD into the correct drive. Close AutoPlay if it appears. If the Burn a Disc box opens, click on **Cancel**.
2. Open **My Computer** from the **Start** menu.
3. Right-click on the icon for **DVD RW Drive** (A in Fig. 24).
4. On the drop-down menu, click on **Format** (B).
5. The **Format DVD RW Drive** (C) box is displayed. Click on **Start** (D).
6. A warning appears reminding you that formatting will erase all data on the disc. Click **OK** to continue, **Cancel** to quit.
7. A progress bar appears while formatting takes place. A date is automatically entered into the **Volume label** (E) box.

*Note: the format drop-down menu can also be used to erase files from a disc; click **Erase this disc (F)**.*

Section 14:
Burn/Copy a File or Folder to a Formatted CD or DVD

1. Insert the CD/DVD into the correct drive in the computer.
2. In an Explorer window, click on the files or folders (A in Fig. 25) to be copied.
3. Click on **Burn** (B) on the command bar.
4. A progress bar appears while the files are copied.
5. Click the **Eject** button (C) and then remove the disc from the drive.

Section 15:
Burn/Copy a File or Folder to a Blank CD or DVD

1. Insert the CD/DVD into the computer and the AutoPlay box automatically appears.
2. Click on **Burn files to disc** (A in Fig. 26).
3. The **Burn a Disc** dialog box will appear.
4. Type in a name for the disc or keep the date already entered (B).
5. Click the option button next to **Like a USB flash drive** (C).
6. Click **Next** (D) and Windows will format the CD/DVD – interrupting this process will corrupt the disc and make it unusable.
7. When the AutoPlay box reopens, click on **Open folder to view files**.

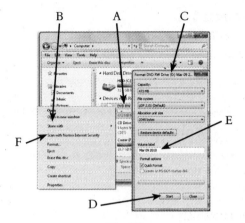

Fig. 24

Fig. 25

8. Highlight the files or folders (A in Fig. 27) that you wish to copy.

9. Click on **Burn** (B) on the command bar and the files will be copied onto the disc.

*Note: if you are planning to use the disc in a CD or DVD player, at step 5 click on the option **With a CD/DVD player**.*

Section 16:
Open a File or Folder on a CD or DVD

1. Insert the CD/DVD into the correct drive in the computer.

2. Click on **Computer** in the navigation pane.

3. Click on the **DVD RW Drive** (C in Fig. 27) and the files on the CD/DVD appear in the contents pane.

4. Double-click on a file and it will open in its relevant program.

Deleting Files and Folders from a CD or DVD

1. Insert the CD/DVD into the correct drive in the computer.

2. When the AutoPlay box opens, click on **Open folder to view files**.

3. Right-click on the file to be deleted and from the drop-down menu click **Delete**.

4. To erase the disc completely, locate the name of the disc in the navigation pane, right-click and from the drop-down menu select **Erase this disc**.

Note: when you delete files from a disc they are NOT placed in the Recycle Bin but are erased forever.

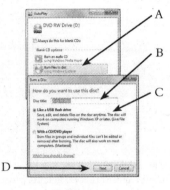

Fig. 26

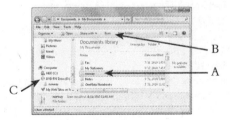

Fig. 27

Chapter Five:
Getting Help and Using Search

Section 1:
Help on Windows 7

Windows 7 provides plenty of help in getting to know the system and sorting out problems. The **Help and Support** centre is simple to use, full of useful information and tutorials and, very importantly, it's easy to find.

Open the Windows Help and Support Centre
1. Go to the **Start** menu and click on **Help and Support**.
2. Windows Help and Support opens.
3. At the top is the **Search Help** text box (A in Fig. 1).
4. Or you might wish to choose from the following tutorials listed under 'Not sure where to start?' (B):
How to get started with your computer
Learn about Windows Basics
Browse Help topics
5. Click a tutorial and you will be presented with a list of subjects (A in Fig. 2) to choose from.
6. Click on the link **Windows** (C in Fig. 1) below 'More on the Windows website' for further help and information. An Internet Explorer window will automatically open; if you are on dial-up you will need to connect to the Internet.

*Extra: take time out to browse through the subjects in **Help and Support** – it's a great way to discover more about Windows 7 and it comes in 'bite-size' chunks which are easy to digest!*

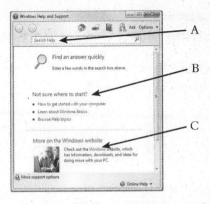

Fig. 1

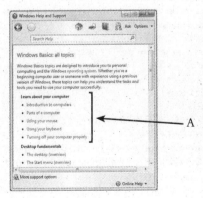

Fig. 2

Section 2:
Getting Help using the Search Box

1. Type the name of your query or subject (A in Fig. 3).
2. Click on the magnifying glass (B).
3. **Help and Support** displays the best 30 results.
4. By clicking on a result further information is displayed.
5. If the information is not what you require then return to the best 30 results again. Try another result. Use the Forward and Back buttons (C) to navigate between pages.
6. Print the information by clicking on the **Print** button (D).
7. For more information available click on **More support options** (E).
8. Click on the **Close** button to close the window.

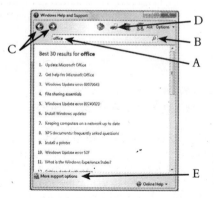

Fig. 3

Section 3:
Finding Help on Specific Windows and Dialog Boxes

A **Help** button (A in Fig.4) is present on the Windows menu bar. (The menu bar is not shown by default; if it has not been selected already, click on Organize on the command bar, then Layout and click to select Menu bar.) A **Help** question mark (B) is also present on most windows and dialog boxes. Click either the Help button or the question mark to open Windows Help and Support, which will list relevant topics relating to the Windows Explorer you are using.

Fig. 4

Section 4:
Searching for a File or Folder

With all the files and folders that can be held on your computer the Search feature is a very useful and easy-to-use tool to quickly find a mislaid item. A search can be made of the whole computer by using Search on the Start menu. Alternatively, a search can be narrowed by searching a specific location such as a folder or library.

Running a Search from the Start Menu

1. Click on **Start** and then in the **Search programs and files** box (A in Fig. 5).
2. As you type the first letters of a word, Windows 7 will search to find a program, folder or document matching those letters (B).
3. The Start menu displays a list of files and folders, sorted into categories, and containing the name of your search (C).
4. Click on an item from the list and the file will open in its relevant program.

Searching a Specific Location in Windows Explorer

1. Decide which sort of file you are looking for, i.e. a document, music or photo, etc., and then open the relevant explorer library window.
2. Click in the Search box and type in a search word, i.e. the name or part of the name of the required file (A in Fig. 6).
3. As you type, results that match your search word within that particular library (B) are listed in the contents pane. Folders containing a match for the search are highlighted (C) while single files are shown with highlighted text (D).
4. Double-click a file or folder to open.

Section 5:
An Advance Search

The advance search on Windows 7 has been streamlined and made more effective with a variety of filters that enable you to narrow down a search. If a file is not found using

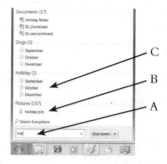

Fig. 5

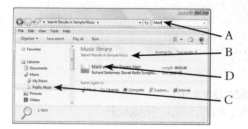

Fig. 6

one type of filter, then try others. The filters vary according to the Explorer window that you are using.

1. Click on a library, folder or other location in the navigation pane.
2. Click in the Search box and a drop-down menu displays the filter options, which will vary depending on which Explorer window you are using.
3. Select a filter option and type in a search word, i.e. the name or part of the name of the required file or folder.
4. The filter you have chosen will narrow the search.
5. The example used in Fig. 7 and 8 is a search in the Pictures library using the filter **Date taken** (A in Fig. 7). Click to select a date or date range (B in Fig. 8).

Here are some examples of different Explorer windows search filters.
Pictures: Date taken, Tags, Type.
Documents: Authors, Type, Date Modified, Size.
Music: Album: Artists, Genre, Length.

Closing the Search Box
Click on the cross at the end of the Search box and the previous search is cleared (A in Fig. 8).

Section 6:
Saving a Search

1. Once you have searched and found a file you can save the search by clicking on the **Save Search** button (C in Fig. 8) on the command bar.

2. A new window opens. Type in a name for your search.
3. Click the **Save** button.

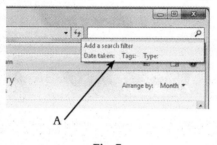

Fig. 7

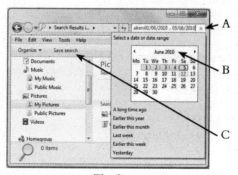

Fig. 8

Open a Saved Search

1. Click on **Favorites** in the navigation pane.
2. Locate and click on the name of the saved search and the search results open in the contents pane.

Chapter Six:
Creating Documents Using
WordPad

Windows 7 comes with a word processing program called
WordPad which allows you to create, format, print and
save the documents.

Section 1:
Getting Started

Opening WordPad
1. Click on the **Start** button, on **All Programs**, and then
on **Accessories**.
2. In the Accessories folder click on **WordPad** and the
WordPad window opens displaying a new page.

Note: type **WordPad** *into the Start menu Search box and it
will appear on the Start menu. Click on it to open. If you use
WordPad on a regular basis it may be useful to pin it to the Start
menu or taskbar.*

The WordPad Window
Open WordPad, click once on the page and the **text cursor**
(A in Fig. 1) appears indicating the place where the text will
appear. Move the mouse pointer over the white page and it
will change from an arrow into an **I**. This shape is called an
I-beam (B). When you're not typing it blinks to show its
position on the page. When the mouse pointer is moved

off the page it reverts to the arrow pointer. The vertical **scroll bar** (C) is on the right-hand side of the page. This will appear when sufficient text has been typed or if you press Enter on the keyboard to move the text cursor down the page. The **title bar** (D) at the top of the page shows the name of the document. The **status bar** (E) appears across the bottom of the window and the **ruler** (F) across the top of the page.

*Note: **Minimize, Maximize and Restore** are functions which are described in Chapter Two, Section 10.*

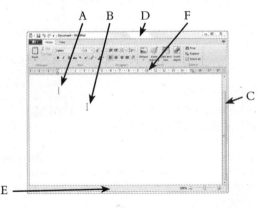

A   B   D   F

C

E

Fig. 1

Fig. 2

Display the Ruler and Status Bar
1. Click on **View** (A in Fig. 2) on the menu bar.
2. Click to place a tick in the check boxes next to each item that you wish to be displayed (B).
3. To remove an item, click the check box to remove the tick.

Section 2:
Moving around the Page Using Keyboard Functions

The keyboard, as well as the mouse, allows you to interact with the computer and to move text and the cursor around the page. See Fig. 3 for the following:

Space Bar: (D) puts a space between characters nd moves the text cursor.

121

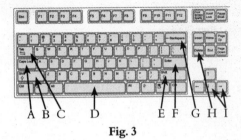

Fig. 3

Enter: (F) moves the text cursor down the page.

Delete: (H) removes text to the **right** of the text cursor.

Backspace: (G) removes letters to the **left** of the text cursor.

Caps Lock: (A) allows you to type continuously in capital letters.

Shift: (B and E) enables typing of single capital letters.

Tab: (C) allows you to create paragraphs, columns and matching spaces in a document. It creates a bigger space than the space created by pressing the space bar.

Cursor Keys: (I) move the text cursor to the top or bottom of the page and to the right or left. They will only work when there is text on the page.

Section 3:
Creating Text

1. Make sure you are looking at a blank page. If you cannot see the text cursor, click once on the page and it will start to blink.
2. Type your text.
3. When the text cursor reaches the end of a line it will automatically move down the page and go to the beginning of the line. This is called wrapping.
4. To move the text down the page before reaching the end of a line press the **Enter** key.

Removing Text Using the Delete Key
1. Move the I-beam to the *beginning* of a line of text.
2. Left-click once and the text cursor moves to the same place.
3. Press the **Delete** key once and a letter from the **right** of the cursor is deleted.
4. Keep pressing the **Delete** key and all the text is deleted.

Removing Text Using the Backspace Key
1. Move the I-beam to the *end* of a line of text.
2. Click once with the left mouse button and the text cursor moves to the same place.
3. Press the **Backspace** key once and a letter is removed from the **left** of the cursor.
4. Keep pressing the **Backspace** key and all the text from on the left of the cursor is deleted.

Typing Capital Letters

To type capitals use the **Capitals Lock** key or the **Shift** key.

1. Press the **Caps Lock** key and all the text you type will be all capitals.

2. Press the **Caps Lock** key once to return to lower case.

3. To type a single capital, press the **Shift** key, hold it down and type the letter.

4. Release the Shift key to return to lower case.

Extra: to type brackets, press and hold down the Shift key at the same time as typing the bracket.

Section 4:
Highlighting Text

Before changing, moving or deleting text it must be highlighted.

1. Click on the Home tab (A in Fig. 4). Type a single line of text. Move the I-beam to the left or right of the text, click with the left mouse button and drag it across the text and the words will be highlighted (B).

2. Release the mouse button.

3. Make any changes you wish. Click once to remove the highlight.

Highlight a Whole Document

1. Click on **Select all** (C) and the whole document is highlighted.

2. Make any changes that you wish.

3. Click once on the page to remove the highlight.

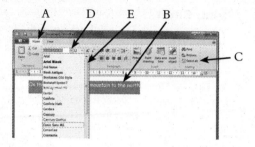

Fig. 4

Extra: to highlight a single word, place the I-beam onto the word and double-click.

Section 5:
Formatting Text

Click on the **Home** tab (notice the text cursor becomes an arrow) to view the formatting tools that will help you to create interesting and colourful documents. As the arrow rests on each tool, it becomes highlighted and the name of the tool is displayed. These tools allow you to change the style (font) and size of the text and to select ways of emphasising what you have typed.

Choose a Style or Font of Text

1. Type a line of text, highlight. Click on the arrow by the **Font Style** (D in Fig. 4) box and a drop-down list shows the numerous styles available.

2. Select a font style – use the scroll bar (E) to see more – click once and the text will change to the new style.

3. When you discover a style that you like, to save time highlighting, select the font *before* you start typing your text.

Choose a Size of Text

1. Click on the arrow by the **Font Size** box (A in Fig. 5). (Size 12 is one of the most frequently used for documents.)

2. Select a size (B) from the drop-down list.

*Extra: you can quickly change the font size by clicking on the **Grow Font** (C) or **Shrink Font** (D) buttons.*

Bold, Italic and Underline Buttons

B is used to **embolden** text

I is used to make text *italic*

<u>U</u> is used to <u>underline</u>

1. Click the **Home** tab (A in Fig. 6). Highlight your text, click once on **Bold** (B).

2. Click once to remove the highlight. The text is emphasised in bold.

3. To remove the bold format, highlight the text, click once on the Bold button and then once on the page.

4. Use the same method for the Italic (C) and Underline (D) buttons.

Note: all three of these buttons can be used in combination with each other.

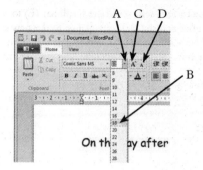

Fig. 5

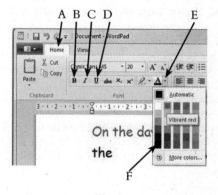

Fig. 6

Using Colour

The **Text Color** and **Text Highlight** buttons enable you to produce eye-catching documents in colour.

Select a Text Colour

1. Click on **Home** tab (A in Fig. 6) and then the **Text Color** (E) button.
2. A drop-down colour chart is displayed (F). Click on the colour you wish to use. Start typing using the new colour.

Changing the Colour of Existing Text

1. Highlight the text that you wish to change and select a colour from the drop-down colour chart.
2. Click once on the page to remove the highlight and the colour of the text will have been changed.

Use Colour to Highlight a Section of Text

1. Highlight the section text that you wish to emphasise and then click on the **Text Highlight Color** (A in Fig. 7) button.
2. Click a colour on the colour chart (B), click once on the page and the text will be highlighted in whatever colour you have chosen.

Remove the Colour Highlight

1. Highlight the text you wish to remove the colour highlight from, click on the **Text Highlight Color** button.
2. Click on **No color,** click once on the page and the highlight is removed.

Section 6:
Moving and Copying Text

The **Cut, Copy** and **Paste** buttons on the **Home** tab (A in Fig. 8) enable you to move text to different places on the page and between documents.

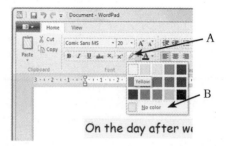

Fig. 7

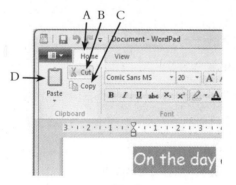

Fig. 8

Copy and Paste

1. Type a few lines of text and highlight them. Click on **Copy** (C in Fig. 8), then click on the place on the page where you wish the text to be copied.
2. Click on **Paste** (D) and a copy of the text is pasted onto the page.

Cut and Paste

1. Type a few lines of text and highlight.
2. Click on **Cut** (B) and the text is deleted.
3. Click on the place on the page where the cut text is to be pasted.
4. Click **Paste** (D) and the line will be pasted into place.

*Note: if you wish to just delete sections of text, use only the **Cut** button.*

Copying Between Documents

You can also copy and paste from one document to another and between different programs. Experiment by creating two documents and type some text on each. Have the first document open on the screen with the second document minimised on the taskbar.

1. Highlight the text on the first document. Click on the **Copy** button.
2. Minimise the first document, and maximise the second document.
3. Click at the end of the text on the second document. Click on **Paste**.
4. The text from the first document will have been added to the second, thus combining the text of both documents.

Aligning the Text

The **Alignment** buttons on the **Home** tab (A in Fig. 9), change the position of the text on the page. Highlight the text and then click on one of the Alignment buttons:

Align Left (B) will arrange text to the left of the page.

Align Center (C) will arrange text down the centre of the page.

Align Right (D) will arrange text to the right of the page.

Line Spacing (E) allows you to alter the space between lines of text.

Note: before you start typing, click on the Alignment button that you wish to use for the document.

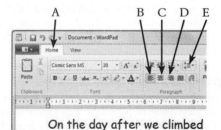

Fig. 9

Section 7:
Opening and Saving a Document

Click on the downward-pointing arrow by the WordPad icon (A in Fig. 10) and a drop-down menu opens showing the tools that allow you to open, save, print and email documents.

Open a New Document

1. Click **New** (B) on the WordPad drop-down menu.
2. Click onto the page to start typing your text.

Saving a Document

1. Click on **Save as** (C). Click on **Rich Text document** (D).
2. Click on **Libraries** (A in Fig. 11) then **Documents** (B) and the library (or a folder within the library) where you wish to save the document.
3. Click in the text box called **File name** (C). Type in a name for the document. Click on the **Save** button (D).

Note: save the document as a Rich Text document (D in Fig.10) in order to retain the font styles, colours and any other formatting used.

Shortcut to Save

1. Click on **Save** (E in Fig. 10).
2. If it is the first time that the document has been saved, the **Save as** box will appear on the screen.
3. If the document has been saved previously it will be automatically saved again in the same location. The **Save as** box will not appear.
4. If you wish to save your document into a different location or do not use this shortcut.

Opening a Saved Document

1. Click on the downward-pointing arrow by the WordPad icon (A in Fig. 10).
2. Click **Open** on the drop-down menu.

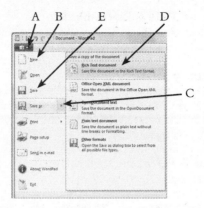

Fig. 10

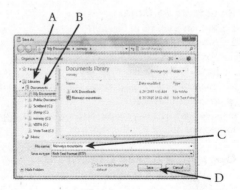

Fig. 11

3. The Open Explorer window opens. Locate the library or folder that contains the WordPad document you are looking for.

4. Double-click on the document to open, or single click and click on the **Open** button.

*Note: to open a document saved in Rich Text Format, click on **All Documents**, select **Rich Text Format (RTF)** and any formatted documents will be displayed in the contents pane.*

Section 8:
Printing

Quick Printing a Document

This is useful when you need only one copy of the document and do not need to make decisions about how many or which pages to print.

1. Point to **Print** on the WordPad drop-down menu.

2. Select **Quick print** and the document is sent straight to your printer for immediate printing.

Note: make sure your printer is switched on and loaded with paper!

Controlling the Printing of a Document

The Print dialog box provides various options, that give you greater control over the printing of a document.

1. Point to **Print** on the WordPad drop-down menu, then click on **Print** on the sub-menu.

2. The **Print** dialog box appears with various options (See Fig. 12).

3. Under **Select Printer** (A), click on the printer that you will be using.

4. Select the **Page Range** (B) by clicking on the appropriate radio button.

5. Specify the **Number of copies** (C): use the spin buttons to increase/decrease the number in the copies box.

6. If you want the pages collated click on the **Collate** (D) check box. (The collate box is only activated when printing more than one page.)

7. When you have finished making your selections, click on **Apply** (E) and then **Print** (F).

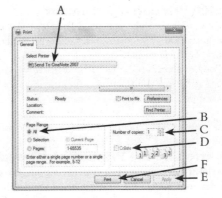

Fig. 12

Print Preview

Print preview allows you to see the layout of the text and to discover any errors that might exist. Corrections can then be made prior to printing.

1. Click on the WordPad drop-down menu.
2. Place your cursor on **Print** and then click on **Print preview**.
3. Print preview opens with a row of tools to enable you to preview your document:

One page or **Two pages** to view
100% to zoom.
Next page and **Previous page** to move between pages
Page setup is a quick link to paper size, orientation and margins

4. Click the **Print** button to print.
5. Click on the **Close** button to return to the original document.

*Note: you cannot make changes to the document whilst in **Print preview**; to do so click **Close** to return to the normal page.*

Section 9:
Laying out the Page

Margins, paper size and orientation are set automatically by the computer. On occasion, however, you may wish to alter these.

1. Click **Page setup** on the WordPad drop-down menu.
2. The **Page Setup** dialog box (see Fig. 13) opens displaying three sections: Paper, Orientation and Margins.

3. The **Preview** (A) reflects changes made to the settings.
4. When you have finished making changes to the settings click on the **OK** button and the changes will be saved.

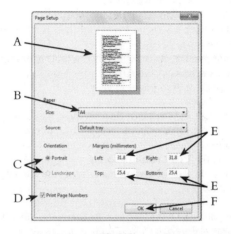

Fig. 13

Choosing a Paper Size

Click on the downward-pointing arrow by **Size** (B) and then on the size you wish to use. A normal document is A4 but if you are printing labels or envelopes you can select one of the other options.

Selecting Orientation

Select the orientation of your document by clicking on either **Landscape** or **Portrait** (C).

Landscape changes the preview page to horizontal.
Portrait changes the preview page to vertical.
The **Preview** (A in Fig. 13) reflects which one you choose
and so helps you to decide which is best for a particular
document.

Print Page Numbers

Click the check box (D in Fig. 13) if you want the page
numbers printed on the bottom of each page.

Changing the Margins

The number boxes labelled **Left**, **Right**, **Top** and **Bottom**
(E in Fig. 13) show the sizes of the margins.

These are set by default, but if you wish to change them,
click into one of the number boxes and type in the size that
you prefer. Look at the **Preview** (A) to see the effect of
changing the numbers and therefore the size of the margins.

Once changes have been made click on **OK** (F).

Section 10:
Adding an Insert to your Document

The **Insert** tool buttons allow you to insert a picture, time/
date, a drawing from the Paint program and other objects
from further programs (see A in Fig. 14). They all follow
the same principle.

Inserting Date and Time

1. Click on the page where the date or time is to be inserted.
2. Click on **Date and Time** (A). Select the format (B)
that you wish to use. Click **OK** (C).

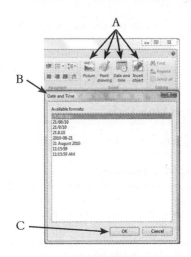

Fig. 14

3. The date or time will be inserted into your document.

Insert a Picture

1. Click on the place in the page where you wish to insert the picture.
2. Click on **Picture** (A). Browse through the Picture library and folders to find a picture.
3. Click on the **OK** button. The picture is inserted.

Insert a Symbol

To insert a symbol or character that is not present on the keyboard:

1. Click on the **Start** button and type into the Search box **character map**. Click on **Character Map** to open.

2. Select a font. Double-click on the character that you wish to insert.

3. Right-click on the word document; click on paste and the character will be pasted into the text.

4. Close the character map when you have finished and return to your document.

Section 11:
Other Useful WordPad Functions

Find

This is useful if you need to find a particular word in a long document.

1. Click on **Find** (A in Fig 15).

2. Type the word you wish to locate into the **Find what** text box.

3. Click on **Find Next** to find the word. Click again to find more.

4. WordPad will tell you when it has finished searching the document.

5. Click **OK**.

Replace

This tool allows you to replace a word within your text with another.

1. Click on **Replace** (B).

2. In the **Find what** text box (C) type in the word you wish to replace.

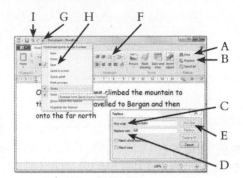

Fig. 15

3. In the **Replace with** text box (D) type in the replacement word.

4. Click on the **Find Next** button (E).

5. Then click on the **Replace** button to replace with the new word.

*Note: to save time click on the **Replace All** button.*

Bullets

Bullets can be used to give emphasis to sections of text in a document.

1. Click on the **Bullets** button (F in Fig. 15) and a bullet appears on the page.

2. After typing a piece of text, press Enter. A bullet is automatically inserted on the next line.

3. To deactivate this function click once on the Bullets button and you will notice that it is no longer highlighted. *Extra: if you wish to use numbering or alphabetise a list, click on the arrow by the bullet icon and then click on the style that you wish to use.*

The Quick Access Toolbar

This sits on the title bar and includes the **Save** and the **Undo** and **Redo** buttons. It can be customised to include more quick shortcuts to functions that you use frequently.

1. Open the Quick Access drop-down menu by clicking on the downward-pointing arrow on the title bar (G in Fig. 15)

2. Click on those items (H) that you wish to include and they will appear on the toolbar.

The Undo and Redo Buttons

The **Undo** button (I in Fig. 15) reverses the last action that you made on the document. The **Redo** button repeats the last action.

The View Tab

1. Click on the View tab (B in Fig. 16). If you want the **Ruler** and/or **Status** bar to be visible click on the relevant check box (A).

2. The **Zoom** (C) buttons allow you to view your page in greater or less detail and to revert back to 100%. You can also move the slider on the status bar to zoom in and out of a page.

3. The **Word wrap** (D) list enables you to select whether to wrap the text of a document to the length of the ruler, the width of the window or to have no wrap at all.

4. The **Measurement units** (E) list allows you to choose which units of measurement you wish the ruler to show – inches, centimetres, points or picas.

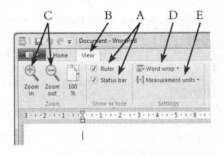

Fig. 16

Chapter Seven:
Personalising your Computer

Windows 7 enables you to alter and personalise your computer settings, add and remove programs, and generally change things to suit your own preferences and requirements. To do this you need to open the **Personalization** window. This can be done through the Control Panel or from the desktop.

Section 1:
Opening the Personalization Window

Opening the Personalization window from the Control Panel

1. Click on the **Start** button.
2. Click on **Control Panel**.
3. The **Control Panel window** opens showing the different functions of the computer grouped together into categories.
4. Click on **Appearance and Personalization** (A in Fig. 1) and then on **Personalization**.
5. Use the **Back/Forward** (B) buttons to navigate between windows.

Users of XP and Vista

There is no longer the Classic View link in the Control Panel; instead to see all the contents of the control pane in alphabetical order, as shown in (C):

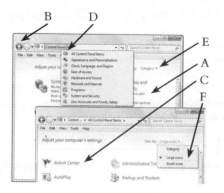

Fig. 1

1. Click on the address bar, then on the drop-down list click **All Control Panel Items** (D).
2. Or click on **View by:** (E) and then on **Large icons** or **Small icons** (F).

Opening the Personalization Window from the Desktop

1. Right-click on an empty section of the desktop (avoid clicking on any icons).
2. On the drop-down menu, click on **Personalize**.

Section 2:
Desktop Backgrounds

Desktop backgrounds have become more interesting! Besides choosing a picture, a slide show or solid colour for your desktop background, you can now also select a theme which is applied to sounds, screen saver, window colour as well as the desktop. You can even create your own theme. While experimenting with different backgrounds, make sure that you can still view some of the desktop as well as the contents of the window. This way you can decide whether you like your selection before you save it

Choosing a Desktop Picture or Colour

1. Open the **Personalization window** (A in Fig. 2). Scroll down until you reach the bottom of the window (B).

2. Click on **Desktop Background** (C).

3. Click on the downward-pointing arrow by the **Picture location** (A in Fig. 3).

Solid Colours – a selection of colours (for extra colours click on **More**).

Windows Desktop Backgrounds – includes a range of pictures.

Pictures library – your own images saved in the Pictures library.

4. Click on **Windows Desktop Backgrounds** and click on a picture, wait a moment and the background changes to the picture you have selected.

5. Use the same procedure if you wish to select a solid colour or an image from your Picture library.

6. Once you have made your choice, click on **Save changes** (B).

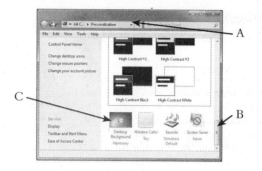

Fig. 2

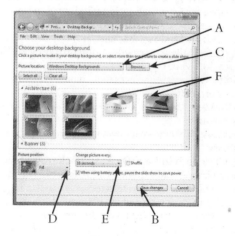

Fig. 3

Importing a Picture or File

Click on the **Browse** (C in Fig. 3) button, click on a folder and the contents will be added to the desktop background files and listed under the folder name.

Positioning Pictures

Click on the arrow below **Picture position** (D) and choose one of the options by clicking on it. Wait as the desktop changes. When you are happy with your selection, click **Save changes** (B).

Create a Desktop Background Slide Show

Use the drop-down list (E) to change the desktop as frequently as you wish. Remove the ticks (F) from those backgrounds you do not wish to include.

Section 3:
Choosing a Theme

You can change the desktop background, window colour, sounds and screen saver all in one go by selecting a **Theme**.
1. Open the **Personalization window**.
2. Click on **Desktop background**.
3. Scroll through the themes (A in Fig. 4) to find one which you prefer – or click on **Get more themes online** (B) if you wish to see more. If you wish to use the earlier style of previous editions, click on **Windows Classic**.
4. Click on the theme you have chosen and the desktop background and taskbar will change immediately. Close the window by clicking on the **Close** button.

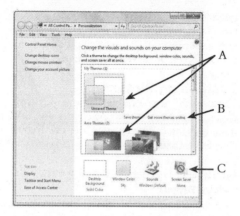

Fig. 4

Section 4:
Choosing a Screen Saver

1. Open the **Personalization** Window and click on
Screen Saver (C in Fig. 4).
2. The **Screen Saver Settings** dialog box is displayed
(see Fig. 5).
3. Click once on the arrow (A in Fig 5) under **Screen
saver**. A drop-down list displays the names of screen
savers.
4. Click on one that appeals and it will be previewed on
the small monitor (B).

5. To see how it looks on the whole screen, click on **Preview** (C). For a few seconds the screen saver will be displayed on the full screen.

6. Once you have decided upon a screen saver click on **Apply** (D) and then **OK** (E).

Changing the Wait Time

The wait time before the screen saver operates can be changed to suit your preference.

1. Locate the box entitled **Wait** (F in Fig. 5).

2. Use the spin boxes to increase or decrease the time before the screen saver is activated.

3. Click on **Apply** and then **OK**.

Note: power management options are covered in Chapter Thirteen, Section 14.

Section 5:
Windows Colors and Aero Glass Effect

The colour of your windows borders, Start menu and taskbar can all be changed to reflect your own taste. The transparency appearance of the aero glass effect can be turned on or off.

1. Open the **Personalization window** and click on **Windows Color**.

2. Click on a colour (A in Fig. 6) and the taskbar and window border will immediately change, previewing your choice. Use the slider control next to **Colour intensity** (B) to adjust the depth of colour.

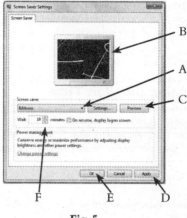

Fig. 5

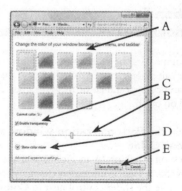

Fig. 6

3. To turn on/off the aero glass effect, click to add or remove a tick in the check box by **Enable transparency** (C).

4. To alter the colour saturation and brightness, click on the **Show color mixer** arrow (D) and then click and drag the slider's controls.

5. Once you have made your various selections, click on **Save changes** (E).

Section 6:
Desktop Icons

Windows 7 enables you to choose and change which items sit on your desktop.

1. Open the **Personalization window** and click on **Change desktop icons** (A in Fig. 7).

2. Click on the check boxes (B) by the icons that you wish to be placed on the desktop – or remove a tick for those icons you do not wish to be displayed.

3. If you wish to change the icon to a different style, click on the icon in the box (C) and then on the button **Change Icon** (D).

4. Select an icon from the display (use the horizontal scroll bar to see more pictures), then click **OK**. Click **Apply** (E), then **OK** (F) on the **Desktop Icon Settings** dialog box.

Change your Account Picture

1. Open the **Personalization window** and click on **Change your account picture** (G in Fig. 7).

2. Choose a picture, click on it and then on the **Change Picture** button.

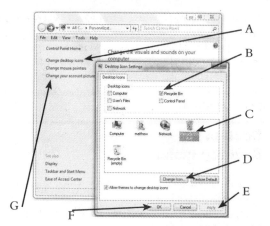

Fig. 7

Section 7:
Sounds, Audio and Volume

Ensure the speakers (or headphones) are attached and the volume controls turned on.

Choosing Sounds to Accompany an Event

1. Open the **Personalization window** and scroll down.
2. Click on **Sounds** (A in Fig. 8). The Sounds tab (B) of the Sounds dialog box opens.

3. Under **Program Events** (C) is a list of events. Some have tiny pictures of loudspeakers adjacent – these events have sounds attached to them. The name of the sound is shown in **Sounds:** (D). If an event does not have a loudspeaker alongside it, **(None)** will show in the Sounds box.

To Change a Sound

1. Click on the event under **Program Events** (C).
2. Click once on the **Sounds:** arrow (D). A drop-down list is displayed.
3. Click on the sound to accompany the event.
4. Click on the **Test** button (E) to hear the sound and if you are happy with it click on **Apply** (F) and then **OK** (G) to save the sound to the event.

Choosing a Sound Scheme

1. Click on the arrow by **Sound Scheme:** (H). Click a scheme.
2. Click any event in the **Programs Events** list (C). Click the **Test** button (E) to preview the sound.
3. When you have made your selection click on **Apply** (F) and then **OK** (G).

To Remove Sounds

1. Open the **Sounds** dialog box, click the Sounds tab. Highlight the event you wish to remove the sound from.
2. Click on the **Sounds**: arrow (D). From the drop-down list click on **(None)**.
3. Click on **Apply** and **OK**.

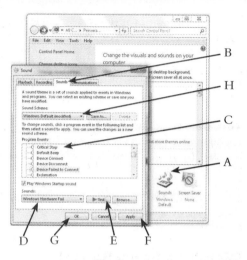

Fig. 8

To Remove all Sounds

Select the **No Sounds** scheme if you wish to remove all the sounds from the computer events.

1. Open up the Sounds dialog box, click on the Sounds tab.
2. Click on the arrow under **Sound Scheme** (H).
3. Click **No Sounds** and then **Apply** and **OK**.

Volume Control

1. Open **Control Panel**, click **Hardware and Sound,** and then on **Adjust system volume**.

2. The **Volume Mixer** box shows the speakers and applications.

3. Click on the slider and drag to adjust to the required volume.

Note: remember to turn on the volume control switches on the speaker controls.

Section 8:
Changing the Appearance of
the Taskbar

1. Open the **Personalization window** and click on **Taskbar and Start Menu** (A in Fig. 9).

2. The **Taskbar and Start Menu Properties** dialog box opens.

3. Click on the Taskbar tab (B). This is divided into three sections:

Taskbar appearance (C)

Notification area (D)

Preview desktop with Aero Peek (E)

4. Under **Taskbar appearance** there are three check boxes: (F)

Lock the taskbar will lock the position of the taskbar on the desktop.

Auto-hide the taskbar causes the taskbar to almost disappear from view – just moving the pointer onto its edge makes it reappear, ready to be used.

Use small icons allows you to reduce the taskbar icon size.

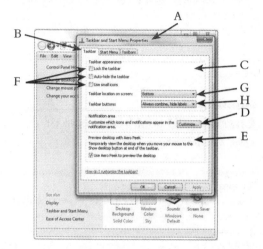

Fig. 9

5. Click on the arrow by **Taskbar location on screen:** (G) and choose whether you wish to place the taskbar at the bottom, top, left or right of the desktop.

6. Click on the arrow by **Taskbar buttons:** (H) to select how you wish the buttons to be combined.

Extra: the taskbar can also be moved into a new position by placing the pointer on a clear part of the bar and then click and dragging it to its new position.

The Notification Area: Process Icons on the Taskbar

This section determines how the icons in the notification area (that's the area to the left of the clock) on the taskbar behave. These icons represent the various processes on the computer and will display notifications about them.

1. Click on the **Customize** button (D in Fig. 9).
2. Locate the icon you wish to modify by scrolling through the list and click on the arrow next to it (A in Fig. 10).
3. Select a behaviour (B).
4. If you want to have all the icons and notifications appear, click on the check box (C).
5. When you have finished making your selections click **OK** (D).

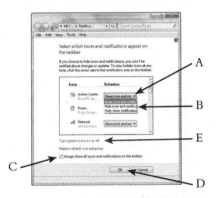

Fig. 10

The Notification Area: System Icons on the Taskbar

The icons of the computer clock, volume, network, action center or power can be turned on or off so that they are visible or hidden on the taskbar. This is an efficient method of keeping the notification area of the taskbar uncluttered. If you turn off an icon, however, you will also turn off any accompanying notification.

1. Click on **Turn system icons on or off** (E in Fig. 10).
2. Locate the icon you wish to turn on or off (A in Fig. 11).
3. Click on the downward-pointing arrow and select **On** or **Off** (B). ('Off' simply means the icon is hidden.)
4. Click **OK** (C).

*Note: to quickly access hidden icons, click on the **Show Hidden Icons** arrow on the notification area, and click on the relevant icon on the menu.*

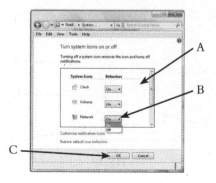

Fig. 11

Preview Desktop with Aero Peek

The third and final section on the taskbar has a check box **Use Aero Peek to preview the desktop** (see E in Fig. 9). If you prefer not to use the Aero Peek option, remove the tick from the check box. If you decide to keep the tick you will be able to use the **Show Desktop** button on the taskbar (see Chapter Two, Section 4).

Section 9:
Personalising the Start Menu

The **Start** button, which sits on the taskbar, is the pathway into the computer and its programs. It can be customised to reflect your own requirements. To do this you need to open **Taskbar and Start Menu Properties**.

1. Open the **Personalization window** (see Section 1 of this chapter) and click on **Taskbar and Start Menu**.
2. Click on the **Start Menu** tab (A in Fig. 12). This tab has a Privacy section (C) and a Customize (B) button.

Privacy and the Recent Items List

In previous Windows versions **Recent items** used to appear by default on the Start menu but in Windows 7 you have to add it yourself.

Adding Recent Items

1. Under the **Privacy** section, click on the check box to add a tick next to **Store and display a list of recently opened programs in the Start menu** (C).

2. Click **Apply** (D) and **OK** (E). Recently accessed files will now be added to the Start menu and provide quick access.

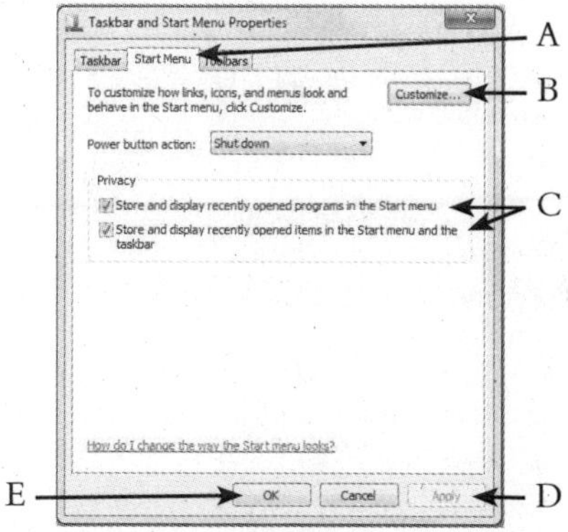

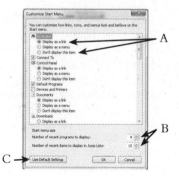

Fig. 12

Fig. 13

Clearing the Recent items list

1. Remove the tick from the check box by **Store and display a list of recently opened items in the Start menu and the taskbar** (C).
2. Click **Apply** and **OK**.

Customising the Start Menu

1. Click on the **Customize** button (B in Fig. 12) and the dialog box called **Customize Start Menu** opens.
2. Click on the relevant radio buttons (A in Fig. 13) as to whether an icon on the Start menu appears as a link or a menu or if you do not want it displayed at all.
3. Use the spin buttons (B) to choose the number of recent programs to display or how many items in display in jump lists.
4. Click **OK** when you have made your selections.

Note: if you decide that you wish to return the Start menu to its original settings then click on **Use Default Settings** *(C).*

Section 10:
Customising the Mouse

The mouse functions can be customised and the clicking speed altered to suit your personal requirements. To do this you need to open the **Mouse Properties** dialog box which has six tabs.

1. Open the **Personalization window** (see Section 1 of this chapter) and click on **Change mouse pointers** (A in Fig. 14). The **Mouse Properties** dialog box opens with six tabs.

2. Click the **Buttons** tab (B) and alter the mouse functions and click speed as described below.

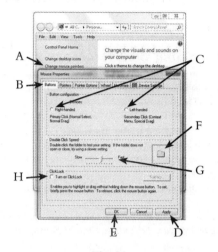

Fig. 14

Swapping Mouse Button Functions

If you are left-handed it may feel more comfortable to change the way the mouse buttons operate. The Button Configuration section (C) shows which buttons carry the primary and secondary functions. If you are left-handed you can switch the functions.

1. Click on an option button to switch the functions of the mouse buttons.

2. Make your selection and then click **Apply** (D) and then **OK** (E).

3. Thereafter when an action requires you to left-click you will need to remember to use the right button, and for a right-click, the left.

Double-click Speed

The computer needs to recognise the difference between a single click and a double-click – a slow double-click will register as two single clicks.

Test Your Clicking Speed

1. Move your pointer onto the yellow folder (F in Fig. 14) and double-click.

2. The folder will open if your double-clicking speed corresponds with the current speed setting. Double-click again to close the folder. If you cannot open or close the folder you can change the clicking speed.

Changing the Double-click Speed

1. Place the pointer on the slider control (G in Fig. 14), left-click and keeping the button depressed drag the slider towards **Slow**. Retest your double-click speed.

2. Adjust the slider control until the folder opens, then click **Apply** and **OK**.

Click Lock (H)

This allows you to highlight or drag without holding down the mouse – useful if you have hand mobility issues.

Mouse Wheels

The **Wheel** tab on Mouse Properties enables you to alter
the number of lines or characters that the central wheel
on the mouse scrolls through at any one time.

1. Open **Mouse Properties** and click on the **Wheel** tab
(A in Fig. 15).

2. Click on the spin buttons by Vertical Scrolling (B) to
alter the number of lines or by Horizontal Scrolling (C)
to alter the number of characters scrolled for every notch
of the mouse wheel.

3. Alternatively, click on the radio button (D) to scroll **One
screen at a time**. Click on **Apply** and then **OK**.

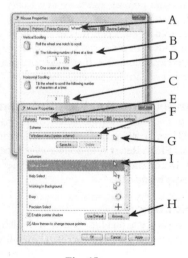

Fig. 15

Section 11:
Customising the Pointers

Using the **Pointers** tab on the Mouse Properties dialog box you can change the style of all or just a few of the pointers. There are large, extra large and magnified styles as well as inverted (black or solid colours rather than white) for those who require a highly visible set of pointers.

To Change the Style
1. Open the **Mouse Properties** box, click on the **Pointers** tab (E in Fig. 15).
2. Click on the arrow by **Scheme** (F). From the drop-down list, choose a style.
3. The pointer style is previewed in the small box in the top right (G).
4. Click **Apply** and **OK** to save the new style.

Changing Individual Pointers
1. To change just a few of the pointers from a current scheme, highlight the pointer listed under **Customize:** (I) and then click **Browse** (H).
2. Scroll through the list. Select a style. Click **Open,** then **Apply** and **OK**.

More Pointer Options
It's possible to vary the pointer speed and trail. Click on the tab called **Pointer Options** which has three sections; Motion, Snap to and Visibility.

Motion

Click and drag the slider between **Slow** and **Fast** until you reach a pointer speed that suits you. Click on **Apply** and then **OK**.

Snap to

Tick the check box **Automatically move pointer to the default button in a dialog box** if you wish to use this feature. Click on **Apply** and then **OK**.

Visibility

1. To experiment with the pointer trail click the check box next to **Display pointer trails**, then move the slider between Short and Long and the pointer will leave a trail. Click on **Apply** and then **OK**.
2. If you do not wish to see the pointer when typing, click the check box by **Hide pointer while typing**.
3. Tick the check box by **Show location of pointer when I press the CTRL key** if you wish to use this feature.

Section 12:
Changing the Date, Time and Time Zone

Changing the Date and Time

1. Right-click on the **date and time** button on the notification area of the taskbar (B in Fig. 16). Click on **Adjust date/time** (A) and the **Date and Time** tab on the Date and Time dialog box opens.

2. To change the time or date click on the **Date and Time** tab (A in Fig. 17) then click on the **Change date and time** button (B). To alter the time use the spin buttons (C) by the digital clock to change the numbers as required and the clock face will reflect the change. Click **OK** (D).

3. To alter the date, click on the date you wish to change to on the calendar (E). To change the month, click on the left or right arrows by the name of the month.

4. Click **OK** (D).

Changing the Time Zone

1. Click on the **Change time zone** button (F) and the **Time Zone Settings box** opens.

2. Click on the down arrow by **Time Zone** and from the drop-down list select the time zone that is applicable. Click **OK**. The computer clock will change automatically to its new setting.

*Extra: make sure the check box by **Automatically adjust clock for Daylight Saving Time** has a tick in it – and you will not have to remember to alter the computer clock.*

Section 13:
Additional Clocks

Two further clocks set in other time zones can be activated and viewed when required.

1. Open the **Date and Time** dialog box.

2. Click on the **Additional Clocks** tab (A in Fig. 18).

3. Click on the required time zone from the list (B).

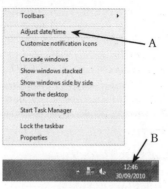

Fig. 16

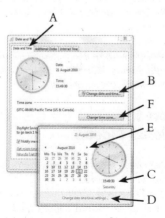

Fig. 17

4. Click to place a tick in the check box so that the clock will be shown (C).

5. Type in a display name for the clock (D). Click on **Apply** and then **OK**.

Viewing the Additional Clocks

1. In the notification area, place your pointer lightly over the digital clock. The clocks and date will briefly appear in digital format.

2. Left-click on the digital clock in the notification area and the clocks and the calendar are displayed. Click on a blank part of the desktop to close. This view has the link called **Change date and time settings** which is another route to open the Date and Time dialog box.

Section 14:
Viewing, Installing and
Removing Fonts

Windows 7 offers a variety of pre-installed fonts (styles of text) to use and the facility to view them and to see how they look in different sizes. You can also print an example or remove a font.

Viewing Fonts

1. Open Control Panel, click on **View by:** and select **Large icons**. Click on **Fonts**. The **Fonts** window opens listing a variety of font styles.

2. Click on a style (A in Fig. 19), then on the **Preview** button (B).

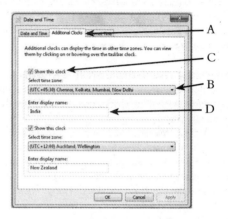

Fig. 18

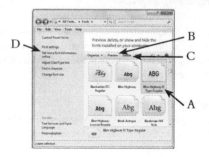

Fig. 19

3. Another window opens displaying the font. If you wish to print a copy of the style, click on the **Print** button.

Deleting a Font

1. Open the **Fonts** window as above and click on the font you wish to remove. Click on the **Delete** button (C in Fig. 19) on the command bar.

2. A **Delete Fonts** box appears. Click on **Yes** if you are absolutely sure that you wish to remove this font or **No** if you wish to keep it.

*Extra: click on **Get more font information online** (D) to discover more.*

Section 15:
Keyboard Properties

Keyboard Properties allows you to decide the pace at which letters appear on the screen and the rate at which the pointer blinks.

Opening Keyboard Properties

1. Open Control Panel, click on **View by:** and select **Large icons**.

2. Click on the keyboard icon (A in Fig. 20). There are two tabs on **Keyboard Properties** dialog box.

3. Click on the **Speed** tab (B).

Altering the Character Repeat Rate

The character repeat rate dictates the speed at which a character (i.e. letter, number, etc.) is displayed when you press and hold down a key. The Repeat delay dictates the delay in time before the character starts repeating.

1. Click in the white text box (C) and then hold down a key to find the speed at which it is repeated.

2. Click and drag the Repeat rate slider (D) to a level that you find comfortable.

3. Do the same for the Repeat delay (E). When you are happy with your choice of speed, click on **Apply** and then **OK**.

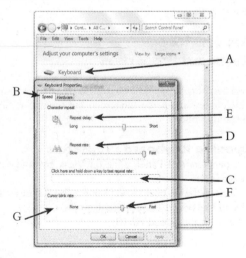

Fig. 20

Altering the Cursor Blink Rate

1. To adjust the rate at which the cursor blinks, click and drag the slider under **Cursor blink rate** (F in Fig. 20).
2. To the left of the slider is a cursor which will reflect the rate that you choose (G).
3. Click on **Apply** and then **OK**.

Note: be aware that if you select a very slow rate (or none at all) it may not be easy to locate the cursor amongst the text in a word document.

Section 16:
Creating Shortcuts

It's useful to create shortcuts to programs and files that you frequently use. Shortcuts sit on the desktop in the form of an icon. When you double-click the icon the program or file will open immediately.

Create a Library, Folder, File or Document Shortcut

1. Open Windows Explorer.
2. Right-click on the library, file, document or folder which requires a shortcut (A in Fig. 21) and a menu opens (B).
3. Click on **Send To** (C) on the drop-down menu and then on the sub-menu click on **Desktop (create shortcut)** (D).

Control Panel

Shortcuts can be created for various programs found in the Control Panel.

1. Open **Control Panel** from the **Start menu**.
2. Click on a category, e.g. Clock, Language and Region.
3. Right-click a sub-category e.g. Date and Time.
4. Click on **Create Shortcut**.
5. The shortcut icon will be placed immediately on the desktop.

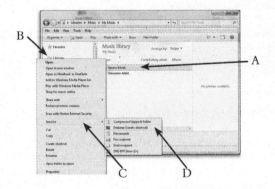

Fig. 21

Section 17:
Removing Shortcuts from your Desktop

1. On the desktop, right-click on the shortcut program icon you wish to remove.
2. Click on **Delete** and the **Delete Shortcut** box will ask you to confirm.
3. Click **Yes**. The shortcut icon is sent to the **Recycle Bin**.

Hiding the Desktop Icons and Gadgets

Instead of deleting all your desktop icons or gadgets it may be convenient for you at various times to hide them – thus giving you a clear desktop.

1. Right-click on a blank section of the desktop.

2. On the drop-down menu, click **View** (A in Fig. 22) and a sub-menu is displayed.

3. To hide an icon or gadget, remove the relevant ticks in the check boxes (B).

4. To view the icons and gadgets again, simply reinstate the ticks.

Extra: the desktop can become cluttered with out-of-date icons, so it's a good idea to regularly delete those which are not longer being used.

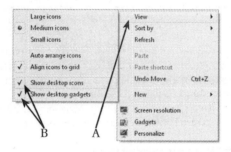

Fig. 22

Chapter Eight:
The Ease of Access Center

The Ease of Access Center groups together settings and tools that make using the computer more accessible for those with certain disabilities. The computer can be adjusted from its default settings to take into account problems with eyesight, speech, dexterity and hearing, and dyslexia. For those with more profound disabilities or with learning difficulties there are various further programs on the market which can be purchased and installed.

Section 1:
Opening the Ease of Access Center

1. Type **Ease** in the Start menu Search box. Click on the program to open. (Pressing the Windows key and U also opens the Center.)
2. The narrator automatically reads aloud as you navigate through the Ease of Access Center. To turn off the narrator remove the tick in the checkbox by **Always read this section aloud** (A in Fig. 1).
3. The Center gives quick access to the Magnifier (B), Narrator (C), On-screen keyboard (D) and High Contrast (E).

Get Recommendations
1. Click **Get recommendations to make your computer easier to use** (F).
2. A set of questions is displayed. Tick the check boxes by the side of those that are relevant. Click on **Next**.

3. When the questionnaire is completed click on **Done**.

4. Windows 7 gives recommendations on what settings to alter, based upon your answers. Decide which are applicable. Activate them by clicking on the relevant check boxes/option buttons.

5. Click **Apply** and then **Save**.

Section 2:
High Contrast

For people who have impaired vision, setting the desktop appearance on a High Contrast theme may make it easier for them to view the various windows and dialog boxes.

1. Open the **Ease of Access Center**. Click on **Set up High Contrast**.

2. On the new window, click on **Choose a High Contrast Theme**. (A in Fig. 2 This opens the **Personalization** (B) window.

3. Scroll down to find the **Basic and High Contrast Themes** (C).

4. Click on one that is appropriate for your needs. If it is not what you want, then try another theme.

Section 3:
The Magnifier

1. In the Ease of Access Center, click on **Start Magnifier**.

2. If the magnifier window changes into a magnifying glass, click on the glass to make it reappear (A in Fig. 3).

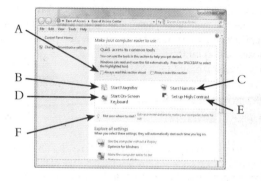

Fig. 1

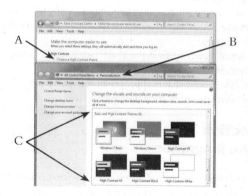

Fig. 2

3. Use the plus and minus buttons (B) to increase or decrease magnification.

4. If you 'lose' the magnifier window it may have minimised into a button on the taskbar. Click to view.

5. To close the Magnifier, click on the **Close** (C) button.

Choose How to Use the Magnifier

1. On the **Magnifier,** click on **Views** (D) and from the drop-down list (E) choose how you want the magnifier to work;

Full screen: enlarges the whole screen

Lens: uses a lens to magnify a section

Docked: a separate window views an enlarged version of the screen

2. Click on the **Options** (F) button to set your preferences.

Zooming: use the slider to increase or decrease zoom (A in Fig. 4)

Turn on color inversion: click to place a tick in the check box to invert colours (B).

Tracking: click the appropriate check box so that the magnifier suits the way you wish to work (C).

3. Click on the links (D) **Fine tune what my screen fonts look like** and **Control whether the Magnifier starts when I log in** to make any alterations that might be useful.

4. Click **OK.**

Section 4:
The On-Screen Keyboard

1. In the **Ease of Access Center** click on **Start On-Screen Keyboard**.

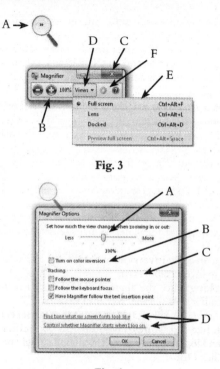

Fig. 3

Fig. 4

2. The keyboard appears on screen.
3. Open a word program in the normal way (A in Fig. 5).
4. Use the mouse to click the keys and your text will appear on your document page.

181

5. If you have problems clicking the mouse you can choose to just hover the mouse over the keys.

6. To do this and make other changes in how the keyboard operates click on the **Options** key (C).

Options

1. Click on the check box (A in Fig. 6) to enable a click sound to be made when the keys are used.

2. Click the check box to turn on the numeric key pad (B).

3. Click on the Hover option button (C) to use the hover feature and then move the slider control (D) to select the length of time the mouse hovers before the key is typed.

4. Click the text prediction boxes (E) to get the tool to list predicted words (B in Fig. 5) as you type. If one of the words is the one you are in the process of typing, click on it to enter onto the document.

5. Click on the links (F in Fig. 6) **About the On-Screen Keyboard** and **Control whether the On-Screen Keyboard starts when I log in** to make any alterations that might be useful.

6. Click **OK** to save your selections.

*Extra: **the On-Screen Keyboard** can be used in conjunction with the magnifier to increase the size of the keys.*

Section 5:
The Narrator

The Narrator can assist by reading out text as you type or by reading aloud on-screen instructions. It works with

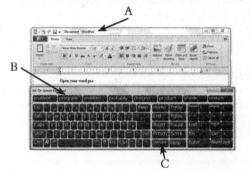

Fig. 5

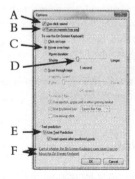

Fig. 6

Notepad, WordPad, Internet Explorer, Control Panel and with the Windows Desktop and set-up.

To Activate the Narrator

1. Open the Ease of Access Center. Click on **Start Narrator**.
2. The **Narrator** box will appear and the narration will begin.
3. Under Main Narrator Settings (A in Fig. 7), click the check boxes that apply.
Echo User's Keystrokes: enables you to hear what you type
Announce System Messages: allows you to hear computer background events
Announce Scroll Notifications: announcement given when the screen is scrolled
Start Narrator Minimized: this minimises the narrator dialog box.
4. To close the narrator click on **Exit**.

Narrator Voice Speed

If you find the voice of the narrator too fast or too slow, click on **Voice Settings** (B). Select a speed from the **Set Speed** drop-down list. In the same way you can also set the volume and pitch to your liking.

Section 6:
Setting up Speech Recognition

Speech recognition is a tool that can read back your text and will repeat each key stroke. Anyone who has visual

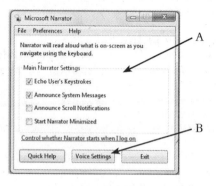

Fig. 7

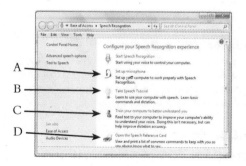

Fig. 8

problems can produce text and control programs within the computer, all by voice. You can click on the speaker symbol in the bottom right hand corner of the taskbar and use the slider controls to adjust the volume.

1. Make sure you have plugged in your microphone.

2. Type **speech** in the Start menu Search box. Click on **Speech Recognition**.

3. Click **Set up microphone** (A in Fig. 8) and the wizard will guide you through a series of instructions.

4. Click **Take Speech Tutorial** (B) to learn how to control the computer using voice commands.

5. Click **Train your computer to better understand you** (C) to learn how to train your voice to communicate effectively with the computer.

6. Click **Open the Speech Reference Card** (D) to print a list of common commands to keep handy.

Chapter Nine:
The Accessories Folder

This folder contains a variety of programs which have been designed for very specific tasks.

Opening the Accessories Folder

1. Click on the **Start menu**, then on **All Programs**.
2. Click on **Accessories** (A in Fig. 1) and the programs are displayed.

Fig. 1

Section 1:
The Calculator

The Windows 7 calculator works in the same way as a hand held calculator. The Standard offers basic functions, while the Scientific is more versatile.

1. Open **Accessories,** Click on **Calculator**. This opens the **Standard** calculator.

2. To open the **Scientific** calculator, click on **View** (A in Fig. 2) on the calculator menu bar and click on **Scientific** (B) from the drop-down menu.

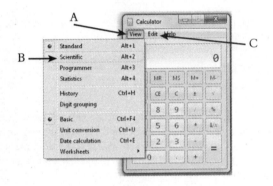

Fig. 2

Pasting the Results of the Calculator into a Document

1. Complete your calculation, click on **Edit** (C) on the menu bar and select **Copy**.

2. On the menu bar of your word program, click on **Edit**, then on **Paste** and your calculation will be entered into the document.

Using the Keyboard to Operate the Calculator

The **numeric keypad** (see Chapter Two, Section 7) on the keyboard can be used to enter information into the calculator.
1. Press the Num Lock key to switch on the number lock.
2. On the main keyboard, use the + key for add, - for minus, ★ for multiply, / for divide and the Enter key for =.

Extra: click on **Help** *on the calculator menu bar to learn more about using the calculator.*

Section 2:
The Snipping Tool

Use the snipping tool to capture images of what's happening on screen – this could be a full screen, or a piece of an image from web pages, word documents, desktop screen savers, pictures or photos, or anything that is currently open on your desktop.

Open the Snipping Tool

From the All Programs list in the Start menu, open the **Accessories** folder and click on **Snipping Tool**.

Capture and Save an Image

Before you capture an image in a 'snip', choose a snipping shape.
1. Click on the down arrow by **New** (A in Fig. 3). Select a shape from Free-form, Rectangular, Window or Full-screen snip (B).

Free-form Snip or Rectangular Snip: Left-click on the screen and keep the mouse button depressed. Drag a shape around the area to be captured. Release the button.

Window Snip (for a program window) or Full-screen Snip: Click anywhere on the screen. The image is automatically captured and enclosed by a coloured box.

2. Once you have chosen the snipping shape the screen will dim and the cursor will change shape to a cross; as soon as you start dragging the cross over the screen the snipping tool will disappear.

3. Release the mouse and the snipped image (A in Fig. 4) will be displayed in the snipping tool.

4. To save the snip, click on **File** (B) then **Save as** (C) and type in the name of the image. Click on **Save**.

5. Use the other tools on the toolbar to copy, email, highlight or erase text, and change pen colour.

Section 3:
Paint

Paint can be used to create artwork, or to edit photos and other images.

Open Paint

1. From the All Programs list in the Start menu, click on the **Accessories** folder, and then on **Paint**.

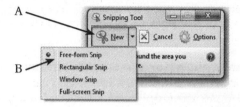

Fig. 3

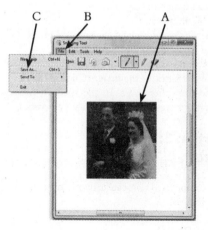

Fig. 4

2. On the **Home** tab (A in Fig. 5) there are a variety of tools to help you create your art work. Hover the pointer over each tool and a box will appear displaying its name.

Tools (B):
Pencil – draw freehand, choose from a variety of line thicknesses
Fill with colour (paint pot) – fill shapes with colour
Airbrush – create an airbrush effect
Magnifier – zoom in on your artwork
Eraser – rub out mistakes
Text – insert text into your picture

Pick a colour (C) – choose a colour before selecting a brush or pencil. **Color 1** determines the foreground colour, **Color 2** the background.

Brushes (D): Click on the downward arrow and select a brush style.

Size (E): Click on the downward arrow to select a size or thickness of line for a brush, shape or pencil.

Shape (F): Choose from a variety of shapes such as stars, squares, arrows, and hearts. Use the Shapes scroll bar to see more.

Shapes and Colour: Creating a Shape
1. Click on a shape.
2. Choose an outline style for your shape by clicking on the down arrow by **Outline** and making a selection.

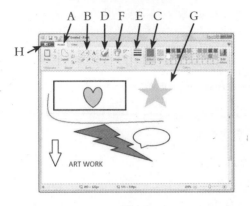

Fig. 5

3. Choose the thickness of the shape's outline by clicking on the down arrow by **Size** and make a selection.

4. Left-click on the drawing area (G in Fig. 5); hold down the button and drag, until the shape is the required size.

Colour outline: Click a shape, click on **Color 1** and then a colour on the palette. Draw your shape on the drawing area.

Fill a shape with colour: Click on a shape, click on downward arrow by **Fill**, and then on **Solid color**. Click **Color 2** and then a colour on the palette. Now draw your shape on the drawing area.

Change a shape's colour: Click on **Color 1,** click on a colour on the palette. Click the **Fill with color** icon in the tools section (B in Fig. 5), and then click the shape on the drawing board and the colour will change.

Change the colour of the drawing area : Click
Color 1, click a colour on the palette, click the **Fill with
color** icon in the tools section, then click on the drawing
area and the colour will change.

The Clipboard
Use the tools on the clipboard (A in Fig. 6) to Cut, Copy
or Paste in the same manner as described in Chapter Six,
Section 6 for a WordPad document.

Adding Text
1. Click on the **Text** tool – represented by the letter A in
the tools section (B in Fig. 5).
2. Move the pointer onto the drawing area. Left-click, hold
the mouse button down and drag the text box (B in Fig. 6)
that automatically appears, until it is the size you require.
3. Click on the **Text Tools** button and Font sizes and styles
are displayed (C). Select a style and size.
4. If the text box is to be transparent and show the picture
below the text, click on **Transparent** – if not, click on
Opaque (D).
5. Click in the text box and then type in the text (E).
6. If you want to change the text, highlight it first.

Editing an Image
1. Click on the Home tab (A in Fig. 7), click on the down
arrow (D) under **Select** and click on **Select all**.
2. To resize the image, click on the **Resize** button (B)
which opens **Resize and Skew**. Use the buttons (E) and
number boxes (F) to make your alterations. Click on **OK**
to view your changes.

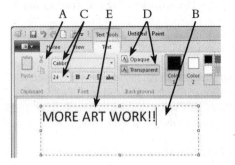

Fig. 6

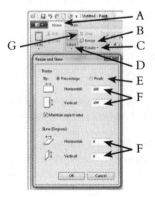

Fig. 7

3. To rotate the image, click on the downward pointing arrow by **Rotate** (C) and make a selection.

4. To invert the colours click on **Select,** and then, from the drop-down menu **Select all** and then on **Invert selection**.

To Save, Open or Print

Click on the Paint menu icon (H in Fig. 5), and select the option you require from the drop-down menu. When saving you need to chose a file type; JPEG or PNG are the most commonly used, with JPEG taking up less computer space.

Customise Quick Access Toolbar

The **Quick Access Toolbar** sits on the title bar of Paint. Click on the downward-pointing arrow (A in Fig. 8) and click to add a tick in the check boxes (B) for any of the functions and they will be added to the toolbar (C).

The View Tab

The View tab (A in Fig. 9) enables you to choose rulers and gridlines to help you with your art work. Click to place a tick in the check boxes for those tools that you wish to use. There is also the magnification feature allowing you to zoom in or out.

Working with Other Images

You can import images from other folders in your computer and then change or add things to them in Paint.

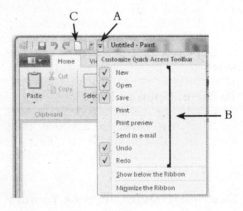

Fig. 8

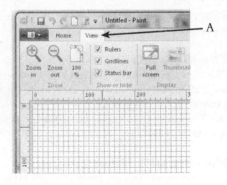

Fig. 9

1. Click on the Paint menu icon (H in Fig. 5), click on **Open** and select your image.

2. If you import a photo or image that is too large click on **Resize** and reduce the percentage size.

3. Use **Skew** if you wish to change the angle of the image or use **Rotate**.

4. If you wish to crop the image/photo click on **Select** and drag the cursor across the section you wish to keep. Click on **Crop** (G in Fig. 7). Only the area you have selected will remain.

5. Click on **Save** to save your image.

*Extra: Paint is a very versatile program and can do many more things than there is room here to describe. Click on the **Help** button to read tutorials.*

Section 4:
Sticky Notes

Sticky Notes can be pasted anywhere on the desktop, in a variety of colours and deleted when no longer needed. Use them as reminders or for making quick notes.

Create a Sticky Note

1. Click on the Start menu, All Programs, and then on the **Accessories** folder.

2. Click on **Sticky Notes** and a note will appear on the desktop.

3. To create a new note, click on the **New Note** button (A in Fig. 10).

Writing, Moving and Deleting Sticky Notes

1. To write on a note, click on it and type your text.
2. To move a note, left-click on the top bar of the note and drag to its new position.
3. To delete a note click on the **Delete** (B) button.

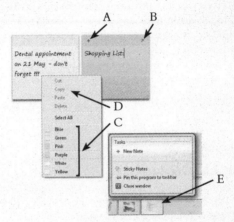

Fig. 10

Change the Colour of a Note

Right-click on a note and select a colour from the drop-down menu (C).

Copying and Pasting Text

1. Highlight the text on the note and right-click on the drop-down menu.

2. Use Copy, Cut or Paste (D) to delete text or add text from another note or from another document.

Hide the Sticky Notes

1. If you wish to hide the notes temporarily, left-click on the Sticky Notes icon (E) on the taskbar This will cause all the notes that are open to be minimised.

2. To make the notes visible again, click once again on the taskbar icon and they will reappear in their original positions.

Section 5:
Windows Journal

Although this program is geared to using a tablet and pen or a touch sensitive computer, text can also be written by keeping the left mouse button depressed while writing. A selection of templates enables you to enter text, create graphs and music and keep a monthly planner.

Open Windows Journal

From the All Programs list in the Start menu, open the Accessories folder, click **Tablet PC** folder, then click **Windows Journal**.

Writing Notes

1. Select a pen shape and colour by clicking on the relevant icons on the toolbar. Enter a name for the note in **Note Title** (A in Fig. 11). Click on to the lined area underneath and write your note.

Fig. 11

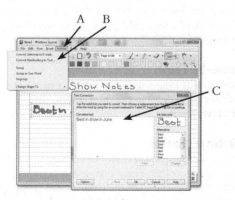

Fig. 12

2. Use the **Tools** (B) on the tool bar to make any alterations – e.g. use the eraser or highlighter or undo buttons.

3. When you have finished, in order to save your work, click on **Save** (E).

Converting Notes to Text

1. Click on the **Selection Tool** (C). Click and drag the box which appears around the notes (D) to be converted.

2. Click on **Actions** (A in Fig. 12) and then on **Convert Handwriting to Text** (B).

3. The **Text Correction** box (C) enables you to make any corrections and click on an alternative. Click **Change** and **OK**.

4. Decide where you wish the text to be placed and click the relevant option button. Click on **Finish** and the notes are converted to text. Click on **Save**.

Altering your Notes

1. Click on the **Selection Tool**. Drag the box around the notes.

2. Click on **Edit** on the toolbar and on the drop-down menu, click on **Format Ink** to change the formatting, colour and thickness of the ink.

Creating Other Types of Notes

Windows Journal contains other types of notes. Choose from graphs, music staff, calendar, shorthand notes, memo and a To do list.

1. Click on **File**, click on **New Note from Template**.

2. Click on a template from the list and then click on the **Open** button.

3. To enter information on the template you have chosen use the same tools as for writing notes.

Printing and Inserting

1. To print your note click on **File** on the menu bar and then on **Print**.

2. To insert a picture click on **Insert** on the menu bar and then **Picture,** select a picture file from your collection and click the **Insert** button. Resize the inserted picture if necessary.

3. To insert a text box click on **Insert** on the menu bar and then on **Text Box**. Left-click and drag the text box to the required size, click inside it and start typing your text.

Section 6:
Writing Text Using the Tablet Input Panel

The **Tablet Input Panel** enables you to write text and insert it into another program, such as a word document or email. Write the text onto the Tablet PC Input Panel using your left mouse button, a touch sensitive computer or a pen and digitising tablet.

Open the Tablet PC Input Panel

1. Click on Start, then on All Programs.

2. Click on the Accessories folder, click **Tablet PC** folder, and then on **Tablet PC Input Panel**.

3. The panel opens on the desktop showing the writing pad button (A in Fig. 13), the keyboard button (B) and the writing pad (G).

Getting to know the Writing Pad

1. Click or tap on the **writing pad** button (A in Fig. 13).
2. Check to see that the correction videos are displayed (E) If not, click on the **Show correction videos** button (F).
3. Click on the correction videos to see how to make corrections, delete, and adding or removing space.
4. Click on **Tools** (C) and from the menu (D) choose either **Write character by character** or **Write in freehand style**.
5. Before you begin to write on the pad, open the program that is going to receive the inserted text e.g. Word document, email, etc.

Writing Text Using Write Character by Character

1. Write each individual letter within the spaces on the line (A in Fig. 14) – as you write the letters are converted into text letters.
2. If a text letter is incorrect, click or tap it and either rewrite or choose from the alternatives (B) offered by clicking on the arrow above the letter (C).
3. Click on **Insert** (D) to enter the text into your program or document.

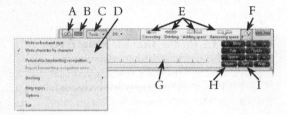

Fig. 13

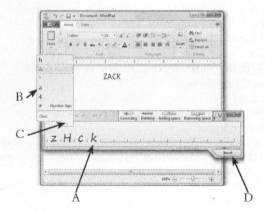

Fig. 14

Writing Text Using Write in Freehand Style

1. Using your left mouse button or pen write freehand on the line on the pad and the letters are converted into text. As you reach the end of a line a new one opens.

2. If a text word is spelt incorrectly, click or tap the misspelt word and either rewrite the letter or use the correction box and select an alternative word. Click on **Insert** (D in Fig. 14) to enter the text into your program or document.

To Insert Numbers or Symbols into your Program

1. Make sure there's no text remaining on the input panel.

2. To insert a number click **Num** (H in Fig. 13) for numbers or **Sym** (I) for symbols.

3. Click on the place in the program where the insertion is to be made.

4. Click on the numbers or symbols required.

5. Click on **Insert** (D in Fig. 14).

The Keyboard Pad

1. Click on the **Keyboard** button (A in Fig. 15) and the panel changes to a keyboard.

2. Click on the place (B) in your program where you want the text to be.

3. Click or tap on individual keys to enter your text.

To Close

1. To send the Input Panel to one side of the screen, click on the **Close** button (C).

2. It can be recalled to the front of the screen by clicking on the edge still visible.

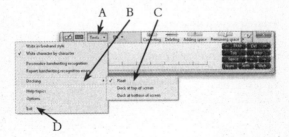

Fig. 15

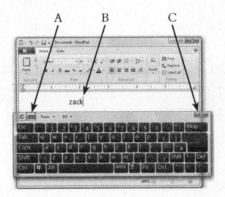

Fig. 16

Docking

Docking allows you to decide where the panel sits on your desktop. You can choose to have it at the top or bottom of the screen or to float.

1. Click on **Tools** (A in Fig. 16) and then **Docking** (B).
2. Select **Float**, **Dock at top of screen**, or **Dock at bottom of screen** (C) by clicking on the appropriate check box.

To Exit

Close the Input Panel, click on **Tools** on the menu bar and then on **Exit** (D).

Extra: to discover more about how to use the Input Panel, click on ***Tools****, then click on* ***Help topics****.*

Section 7:
Math Input Panel

This feature enables you to enter equations and formulae into another program or document.

1. From the All Programs list in the Start menu, open the **Accessories** folder.
2. Click on **Math Input Panel**. Use your mouse or digitised pen to write.
3. Use the keyboard buttons (A in Fig. 17) to write, erase, select and correct, undo, redo and clear. If the buttons are not on display, click on **Options** (B) on the title bar, and from the drop-down menu (A in Fig. 18) click **Show on-screen keyboard buttons**. Select which side of the writing area the buttons are displayed by clicking the appropriate check boxes (B).

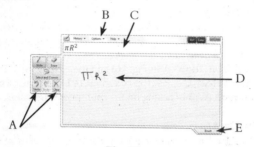

Fig. 17

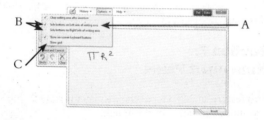

Fig. 18

4. As information is entered onto the pad (D in Fig. 17) it's previewed in the panel above (C).

5. To have a grid on the writing area, click on options (B) then on **Show grid** (C in Fig. 18).

6. Once the maths equation is completed, click on the place in your document or program where you wish it to be inserted and then click **Insert** on the input panel (E in Fig. 17).

Extra: to learn more about the versatility of the Math Input Panel, click on Help on the title bar and work your way through the topics on offer.

Section 8:
Other Accessories

Digitising Tablet and Pen

These are items that give greater versatility in the use of a computer. Write in the normal way on the digital tablet using the accompanying pen and the words will appear on the screen – very useful for those who have problems using the keyboard. They are simple to install and usually come with their own installation CD – many makes also include a tutorial.

WordPad and Notepad

There are two word programs that are housed in the **Accessories** folder: WordPad and Notepad. WordPad is more versatile for creating interesting documents while Notepad is useful for making quick notes which do not require a lot of formatting. Chapter Six covers creating documents using WordPad.

Chapter Ten:
Computer Security and Maintaining Privacy

Section 1:
About Computer Security

When you connect to the Internet to browse the web or to send/receive email there's always the potential risk of harmful programs infecting your computer. It's therefore *essential* that you take precautions to protect your system; especially as new viruses and programs are constantly being created and circulated on the Internet.

Today, Internet providers do a lot to screen for such programs, but all computer users need to play their part by ensuring that the individual security features on their system are activated and kept up to date. Maintaining privacy can also be an issue; Windows 7, Internet Explorer 8 and Windows Live Mail all have features to help you preserve your personal information.

The Threats
There are a variety of infections including spyware, viruses, malware and worms. Malware is so called because it's developed with the intention of doing malicious harm to computers. Spyware are programs that are introduced into your computer via the Internet and without your knowledge or permission. They are used to extract your personal information for illegal use. Other infections,

scams and invasions of privacy can be triggered by opening email attachments, visiting targeted websites or using corrupted CDs/DVDs from an unreliable source.

Many infections are just annoying and not detrimental. There are others, however, that are intentionally designed to corrupt a computer's system and that have the potential to eradicate its contents. Other programs may possibly use your computer as a host, working out of sight and unknown to you, but sending out signals to damage other user's computers. Less dangerous infections can cause your computer to work very slowly, so that using it becomes a chore.

Staying Safe

Before you connect to the Internet, send or receive email or use someone else's CD/DVD/USB memory stick you need to ensure your Windows 7 security features and other programs are set up and working.

Here is a check list to help:

1. Set up your User Accounts and passwords (Section 9).
2. Check that Windows Firewall is switched on (Section 4).
3. Select settings to enable Windows Defender to scan and remove spyware and malware. (Sections 5 and 6).
4. Install and activate an anti-virus program (Section 3).
5. Select your Security options on Internet Explorer (Section 15) and be vigilant against Phishing (Section 12).
6. Choose the level of security for Windows Live Mail (Chapter Twelve, Section 8).
7. Ensure that all the settings you choose are high enough to protect your computer, your privacy and your work.
8. Remain alert to any public announcements of new threats and follow the advice given.
9. Stay up to date.

Section 2:
Avoid Infection – Be Aware!

There are some simple steps that you can take to minimise any possible infections affecting your computer.

Email Awareness

1. Emails from unknown and suspicious sources should be placed unopened in the Recycle Bin and then deleted completely from your system. The emails themselves do not contain viruses – these are in the attachment, and they operate once the attachment is opened.

2. Do not respond to emails from suspicious and unknown sources.

3. Do not disclose any personal information to an email request. Genuine banks, organisations and companies will *never* ask you to do this.

Take Care with CD/DVD/USB devices

1. *Do not* interchange CDs/DVDs/USB memory sticks between home and your place of work as this is a common way of introducing and spreading viruses.

2. If this is unavoidable, scan before using.

Be Website Wise

Some websites are designed purposefully to introduce spyware, viruses or to extract personal information. When shopping or banking online make sure that the site is a secure one. Check by looking at the website address and for the padlock at the top of Internet Explorer (see Section 14).

Back-up Insurance

Use Windows 7 Backup and Restore (see Chapter Thirteen, Sections 4–6) as insurance against your hard drive being corrupted or crashing – it's a way of keeping copies (back-ups) of your files and folders on CDs or memory devices such as external hard drives. The latter can hold a lot of information and are a good investment. If anything bad happens, then you will not have lost all your work.

Be Virus Vigilant

Windows Defender does not protect against viruses and if an anti-virus program does not come as part of the purchase package of your computer then you *must* install one.

Stay Up to Date

Set your firewall and Windows Defender to automatic updates. Be sure to keep your anti-virus program updated as well. As new threats evolve, anti-virus programs continually work to keep pace with the latest developments. When your anti-virus program prompts you to download an update, do so immediately.

Password Precautions

Genuine websites, such as online banks, shops and investment sites, for example, take a great deal of care to make their sites secure and safe to use, very often requiring passwords, user names, number sequences and answers to questions known only to the user. Never give anyone your password or log in details, either verbally or in an email.

It is for *your use only*, to enable you to access the website for which it was designed. If you disclose these details to anyone then your security is seriously compromised. If anyone ever contacts you and requests your log in details immediately contact the company concerned and they will advise you.

Section 3:
Anti-Virus Software and Protection against Viruses

Windows 7 does not include protection against viruses so it is essential that you invest in anti-virus software. Good anti-virus programs are designed to automatically scan your computer at regular intervals and inform you of the virus status of your computer. It will tell you if a virus has been detected and isolate any that it finds. It will also advise you when it's time to update to protect against the latest virus threats.

Sometimes an anti-virus program is included when you purchase a computer package and they often offer a month's free approval. If not, there are a number of anti-virus programs which you can purchase online or from your local computer store. Three of the most popular and efficient are:

Norton Antivirus: www.Norton.com.

McAfee: www.McAfeeStore.com.

AVG: http://free.avg.com/. This site provides a free download version as well as other versions that can be purchased.

Installing Anti-virus Software

1. If you have purchased an anti-virus system as a CD, insert the disc and then follow the instructions that come with it.

2. If you download a program from the Internet, follow the instructions as they appear on the product maker's website.

3. Whichever you choose, the anti-virus software will automatically place an icon on your desktop or on the notification area of the taskbar.

4. Click on either and you will be able to run the program and access its features.

Note: once a program has been added it will become part of the Action Center, which will notify you if and when the program becomes out of date.

Section 4:
Protection against Malware using Windows Firewall

Windows 7 Firewall checks all incoming and outgoing information from the Internet, networks and your computer and either allows it through or blocks it. This helps to prevent worms and hackers from gaining access to your system, and to stop any incoming malware. It also prevents your computer from sending out damaging emails and programs.

Activate Windows Firewall

1. Open the **Control Panel**, and in large or small icons view (A in Fig. 1) click on **Windows Firewall** (B). Use

the **Back/Forward buttons** to help navigate between windows (D). (This is also the route to **Windows Defender** (C) which is described in Section 5.)

2. Windows Firewall will show your settings in green if turned on or red if turned off. A in Fig. 2 shows it turned off.

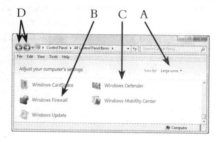

Fig. 1

Fig. 2

3. Click on **Turn Windows Firewall on or off** (B in Fig. 2) and a new window opens.

4. Check that the option buttons next to **Turn on Windows Firewall** have been selected (A in Fig. 3).

5. You can modify the settings by clicking on the check boxes below the option buttons. If you select **Notify me when Windows Firewall blocks a new program** (B), a notification will appear in the notification area on the taskbar when a new program has been blocked. This will enable you to decide whether or not to let a program through the firewall.

6. **Block all incoming connections** (C) should only be used when a serious threat is announced.

7. Click **OK** to save your settings and you are returned to the Windows Firewall window.

When should you block all incoming connections?

There may be occasions when a security alert is issued; these are often reported on news programs on TV and the Internet, especially when a new and insidious software program or virus has been detected.

Until a defence (or patch) has been developed to protect against the virus and sent to all users it may be wise to click on the check box, **Block all incoming connections, including those in the list of allowed programs**.

This setting will block all attempts at connection to your computer; however, you will still be able to view most web pages and use email. Once a patch has been downloaded and installed and/or the alert is over, you can downgrade this increased security level by removing the tick in the check box.

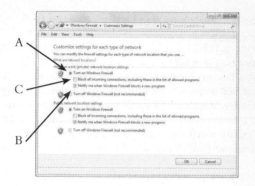

Fig. 3

Important: *there are other firewall programs that can be installed onto your computer but this can cause a conflict if you have both working at the same time. You may need to turn one of them off. But always make sure that one of them is activated.*

Section 5:
Windows Defender: Protection Against Spyware

Windows Defender is a program used to scan and search your computer for any harmful malware or spyware; however, it does not protect against viruses. It works continually in the background, giving real-time protection against any unwanted software that tries to install itself onto your computer or to exploit programs that you have downloaded and use frequently.

219

Open Windows Defender and Check for Updates

1. Open the **Control Panel**, and using large or small icons view, click on **Windows Defender** (C in Fig. 1).

2. The Defender window shows its current **Status** (A in Fig. 4) and the Home (B), Scan (C) and Tools (D) buttons.

3. If Defender hasn't recently been updated the window will also display a button called **Check for updates now** (E). Click on this (connect to the Internet) to receive updated definitions which enable Window Defender to detect the latest threats.

4. A progress bar will appear while Windows Defender checks for updates, downloads and then installs updates.

5. Windows Defender will inform you when updating is completed.

6. Status information will be displayed at the bottom of the window.

7. Windows Defender can also be activated at any time to perform a complete check of your system (see Section 8).

What to do with Suspicious Software or a Possible Infection

Windows Defender will alert you if it finds anything it deems suspicious, and you will be asked to choose whether to quarantine, remove or allow the program.

Quarantine: This prevents the software from running until you decide whether to remove or restore it.

Remove: This deletes the software completely.

Allow: The software is added to the allowed list and Windows Defender will stop alerting you to any risks associated with it.

Windows Defender may quarantine any new software which you have installed and which you know to be harmless. If this is the case the program can be restored and you will be able to run it as normal. For those programs that you do not recognise or you know to be a threat they can be removed.

Restoring or Removing Quarantined Programs

1. Click on **Tools** (D in Fig. 4) and the **Tools and Settings** window opens.

2. Click on **Quarantined items** (C in Fig. 5). Click on **View** and then highlight a program.

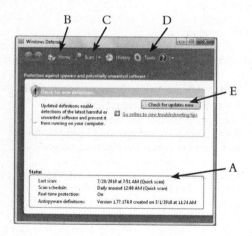

Fig. 4

3. Click **Remove** to delete or **Restore** to allow the program to run.

4. To remove all the programs quarantined click on **Remove all**.

Section 6:
Setting Windows Defender Options for Automatic Scanning

1. Click on **Tools** (D in Fig. 4) to open **Tools and Settings**.

2. Under **Settings**, click on the **Options** button (B in Fig. 5). On the left of the window is a list (A in Fig. 6) of 7 options: Automatic scanning, Default actions, Real-time protection, Excluded files and folders, Excluded file types, Advanced and Administrator.

Automatic Scanning

Windows 7 recommends that you scan your computer daily for risks. This can be set up by Windows Defender so that it occurs automatically at a specific and convenient time.

1. Click on **Automatic Scanning** in the Options list. Select the check box next to **Automatically scan my computer (recommended)** (B in Fig. 6) and further options are displayed.

2. Click on the down arrows to select the frequency of a scan, the approximate time and the type of scan (quick or full) (C).

3. Click on the check boxes to add or remove a tick against **Check for updated definitions before scanning** (D) and **Run a scan only when system is idle** (E).

4. When you have made your selection click on **Save** (F).

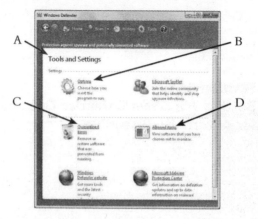

Fig. 5

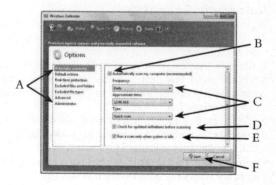

Fig. 6

Section 7:
Setting Windows Defender Options for Security Alerts

Default Actions and Alert Levels

Alert levels are designed to help you to choose how to deal with spyware. Some new software can be benign – it could be part of a licence agreement when installing a new program, for example. Others, however, are potentially harmful, damaging your computer and compromising your privacy. The alert levels are Severe or High, Medium and Low. The threat to your computer can vary from affecting your privacy and damaging your computer to benign software installed with your agreement.

1. Click on **Tools** (D in Fig. 4) and then on the **Options** button (B in Fig. 5).

2. Click on **Default actions** (A in Fig. 7). If you are unsure which settings to choose leave Windows Defender on its default settings of **Recommended action based on definitions** (B).

3. To do this make sure the check box **Apply recommended actions** (C) has a tick in it and then click on **Save** (D).

4. To find out more about Defender Alert levels click on the link, **What are actions and alert levels?** (E).

Real-time Protection

1. Click on **Tools** (D in Fig. 4) and then on the **Options** button (B in Fig. 5).

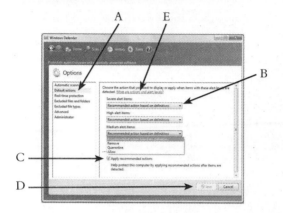

Fig. 7

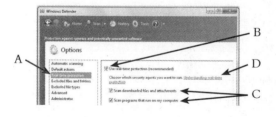

Fig. 8

2. Click on **Real-time protection** (A in Fig. 8). Ensure there is a tick in the check box by **Use real-time**

protection (recommended) (B), which will activate the two check boxes below (C).

3. Ensure there are ticks in these two check boxes – this will mean that Windows Defender will scan files and attachments that you download and programs which you run on the computer. Only remove a tick from these boxes if you *fully understand* the implications of removing them.

4. Click on **Save**.

Extra: to find out more about real-time protection click on **Understanding real-time protection** *(D).*

Excluding Files and Folders from Scanning

Scanning a computer does take time but is vital if you download from the Internet, receive email or use memory sticks and CDs/DVDs provided by other people. However, those files that you personally create may not require scanning. If so, they can be excluded from a Windows Defender scan.

Excluded Files and Folders

1. Click on **Tools** (D in Fig. 4) and then on the **Options** button (B in Fig. 5).

2. Click on **Excluded files and folders**.

3. To exclude a file or folder click on the **Add** button. **Browse for Files and Folders** opens.

4. Locate the required item and click on it to highlight.

5. Click **OK** and the item is added to the excluded list. Click on **Save**.

6. To remove an item from the excluded list, highlight and click on **Remove**.

Excluded File Types

1. Click on **Excluded file types**. To add a file type to the excluded list you will need to type in the text box the file extension or type. For example, a drawing may be in PEG and a photo from your camera may be in JPG.

2. When the file extension has been typed the **Add** button is activated.

3. Click on it and then on **Save**.

4. To remove an item from the excluded list, highlight and click on **Remove**.

Advanced and Administrator

1. Click on **Tools** (D in Fig. 4), click on the **Options** button (B in Fig. 5).

2. Click on **Advanced**.

3. It's advisable to tick all the check boxes under these options.

4. Click on **Administrator** (A in Fig. 9).

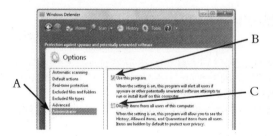

Fig. 9

5. Ensure that the check box by **Use this program** (B) is ticked. This means that all users of the computer will be alerted to potential spyware.

6. If the administrator of the computer wishes to see the History, Allowed items and Quarantined items from other users tick the check box by **Display items from all users of this computer** (C). Be aware that the privacy of other users will not be maintained.

Section 8:
Scanning your Computer for Harmful Software

Use Windows Defender to scan your computer at any time you feel necessary to identify possible harmful infections.

1. Open Windows Defender and click **Scan** on the toolbar.

2. Scanning will begin using whichever options you have previously chosen when setting up Windows Defender.

Scanning Options: Quick or Full Scan

1. A quick scan will take a few minutes while a full scan, depending on your computer, may take over an hour. It's a good idea to do a quick scan at least once a day and a full scan at least once a week.

2. Click on the arrow by **Scan** (A in Fig. 10) and select **Quick scan** or **Full scan** (B) and scanning will begin immediately.

Custom Scan

A **Custom Scan** enables you to scan specific parts of your computer/CDs/DVDs/memory devices.

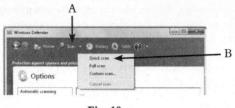

Fig. 10

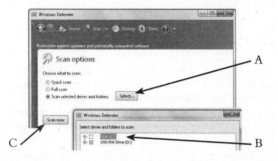

Fig. 11

1. Click on the arrow by **Scan** and select **Custom scan**.
2. Click on the **Select** button (A in Fig. 11) by **Scan selected drives and folders**
3. On the dialog box select the drives and folders (B) to be scanned. Click **OK**.
4. On the Windows Defender window click on **Scan Now** (C).

Scanning Progress and Stopping a Scan

1. A progress bar will appear while scanning proceeds.
2. The window will display details of the scan and the time taken.
3. To stop a scan before it has finished, click on **Cancel** (A in Fig. 12).

Scan Report

1. Scan statistics (B) and a status report (C) will be displayed once the scan has been completed.
2. There is also a button to click to **Check for updates now** (D). If any infection has been detected, Windows Defender will give a report.

Section 9:
User Accounts and Passwords

User Account Control can be used to provide extra security by preventing harmful programs from making changes to your computer without your knowledge. The User Account dialog box will appear when Windows requires your permission to do something. It's a powerful tool against malicious software and during a security alert it's advisable to place it on its highest setting. However, this means that the User Account dialog box will appear with greater frequency and it can become irritating. It's probably safe to reduce the setting when you are working offline and are not connected to the Internet, but always increase it again before going back online. Never place the setting at the lowest level – you will put your computer and

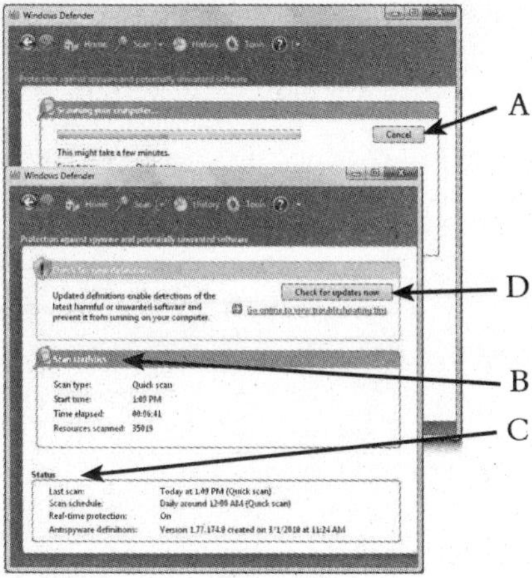

Fig. 12

your personal files at risk. It's a good idea to double-check every so often that the settings have not been lowered.

1. Click on **Start**, then on **Control Panel**, and in large or small icons view click on **User Accounts**.
2. Click on **Change User Account Control settings** (A in Fig. 13).
3. Use the slider control to adjust the settings (B).
4. Click on the link **Tell me more about User Account Control settings** (C) to find out more about how to use the settings.
5. Click **OK**.

Fig. 13

User Account Control Dialog Box

If you are a standard user the User Account Control dialog box will pop up whenever you try to alter settings or download a program. The holder of the Administrator user account will need to enter their password in order for you to proceed. Otherwise you will need to click on Cancel.

Section 10:
Managing Security Alerts Using the Action Center

The **Action Center** enables you to easily manage the security elements of Windows 7. These are: Windows

Update, Internet Security, Windows Firewall, Spyware protection, User Account Control and the additional virus protection system that you have installed. It also has an icon which sits in the notification area of the taskbar. This will flag up any problems that may arise with security and direct you towards solutions.

Messages from the Action Center

1. Hover your pointer over the **Action Center** icon (A in Fig. 14) in the notification area of the taskbar and it will inform you of any messages (B).

2. Click the Action Center icon for details of the messages (C).

3. Click on **Open Action Center** (D).

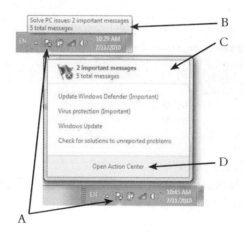

Fig. 14

The Action Center Security Features

In the Action Center window under the heading of Security will be listed any issues that need to be resolved. Anything in red requires urgent attention, orange is a reminder and 'green is good'.

1. To open the Action Center click on the icon on the taskbar.
2. Click on the button by a security problem – it may say **Update now** or **Change settings** or **Get a program online** (A in Fig. 15).
3. Click on the down arrow next to Security (B). The security section expands to list the security features and settings. (You may need to scroll down to see them.)
4. Check that the security features are turned on.
5. If they are turned off or are out of date, click a button to update or a link to get a different program.

Turning the Action Center's Messages On or Off

1. Open the Action Center window.
2. Click on **Change Action Center Settings** (C in Fig. 15).
3. Click the check boxes (A in Fig. 16) by those security features that you wish the Action Center to monitor and send appropriate messages when necessary.
4. It's advisable to keep all the boxes checked to maintain a high level of vigilance.

Fig. 15

Fig. 16

Section 11:
Staying Up to Date with
Windows Update

Viruses, spyware and malware are constantly being developed and new threats being created. It is therefore essential that you keep your system up to date.

1. Open the Action Center window.
2. Click on **Windows Update** (D in Fig. 15).
3. Click on the update links (A in Fig. 17) to view them.
4. Remove the ticks in the check boxes against those updates that you do not require. If you do not use a particular program you would not need the update for it.
5. Click **OK** and then **Install updates** (B). Windows will start to install the updates.

Decide How to Update

1. Open the **Action Center** window.
2. Click on **Windows Updates,** then click on **Change settings**.
3. Click on the downward-pointing arrow (A in Fig. 18) to choose how you wish to update.
4. If you select **Install updates automatically** (B), you can also select the day and time at which this is done from the drop-down lists(C) by **Install new updates**.
Installing updates does slow down the computer, so pick a time when you are not working on it (ensure that it remains switched on and connected to the Internet).
4. If you prefer to select which updates are installed, select one of the other options.
5. Click **OK** to save your settings.

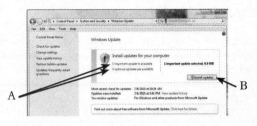

Fig. 17

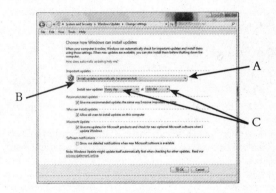

Fig. 18

Section 12:
Protection against Phishing

Phishing is an illegal practice whereby personal information is extracted from unsuspecting Internet users for fraudulent purposes. Such fraudsters may send an email, ostensibly from a reputable source such as a bank, and the recipient is tricked into divulging personal information. This may be either in response to the email or by being directed to a bogus website which requires a visitor to register.

Such 'registration' may ask for details on banking, password, date of birth, mother's maiden name, etc., all of which can be used to remove money from banking or savings accounts or be sold to others in the business of identity theft. **Internet Explorer 8** comes with **SmartScreen Filter** which provides extra protection against phishing.

Turning SmartScreen Filter On or Off

1. Open up Internet Explorer. On the Internet Explorer toolbar click on the **Safety** button (A in Fig. 19).
2. Click on **SmartScreen Filter** (B) and then click either **Turn on SmartScreen Filter** or **Turn off SmartScreen Filter** (C).
3. The **SmartScreen Filter** window opens (as in Fig. 20).
4. Click on one of the option buttons (A in Fig. 20) to turn on or off.
5. Click **OK**.

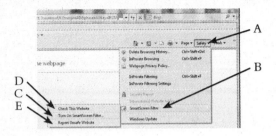

Fig. 19

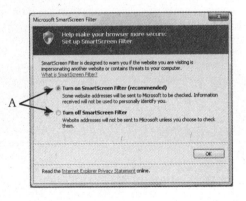

Fig. 20

Check Out a Website for Phishing

If when browsing the Internet you visit a website that is unknown to you, it's a good idea to check to see if it has previously been identified as a 'phishing' site. This is particularly relevant if a site asks you to register first and give personal details before granting you access to the site.

1. While online, click on the **Safety** button on Internet Explorer, and then on **SmartScreen Filter**.
2. Click on **Check This Website** (D in Fig. 19).
3. A progress bar will display while the web address is being checked.
4. A box will appear telling you the result of the search. If all is well click **OK**.
5. A warning will appear if the site is a known or reported phishing site. Do not proceed further but close the web page.

Important: scam emails and websites are always evolving and becoming more sophisticated; genuine companies and financial institutions will not ask for details via email – if they need to contact you regarding personal information they will write a letter. Stay safe – make sure when shopping or banking online that the site is a secure one. Never give away passwords, personal details or information on chat sites.

Reporting a Possible Phishing Site

If a website that you visit makes you suspicious you can report it by clicking on the Safety button, SmartScreen Filter and then on **Report Unsafe Website** (E in Fig. 19). Microsoft website will open. Click the check box next to **I think this is a phishing website** and then click on the **Submit** button.

Section 13:
Managing Pop-ups

Pop-ups are extra windows that 'pop up' when you visit a website; they are often advertisements for things other than the subject of the original web page. They are usually irritating rather than a threat to privacy, but they can sometimes disguise malware or spyware. Internet Explorer blocks pop-ups by default, but unfortunately some legitimate websites will not allow you to view their content unless you allow their pop-ups.

Turn the Pop-up Blocker Off or On

1. On Internet Explorer go to **Tools** (A in Fig. 21) and click on **Pop-up Blocker** (B) and then click either **Turn Off Pop-up Blocker** or **Turn On Pop-up Blocker** (C) – whichever is appropriate.
2. A box will appear asking if you are sure you wish to turn the blocker off or on.
3. Click on **Yes**.

Allowing Pop-ups from Certain Sites

1. On Internet Explorer go to **Tools** and click on **Pop-up Blocker** then **Pop-up Blocker Settings** (D in Fig. 21).
2. Type the address of the website (or cut and paste from the Internet address bar) into the address bar (A in Fig. 22).
3. Click on **Add** (B) and the site will be placed into the **Allowed sites** (C) section.
4. To remove a site from the allowed sites list, highlight it and click on **Remove** (D).

5. Click the check boxes (E) under **Notifications and blocking level** for a sound to be made and/or information bar to appear when a pop-up is blocked.

6. Click on the downward-pointing arrow (F) to select a blocking level from the list.

Section 14:
Online Transactions

Great efforts have been made to increase the level of security for users of online shopping and banking; encoding devices used are of the highest quality and complexity. But be vigilant: always look to ensure that a site is secure and has security certificates.

Checking Website Security

1. On a shopping website the security features will appear once you reach the checkout page. You may also, but not always, be informed that you are entering a secure site. When using a personal banking website you will first be required to log in using the password which you chose when registering for online banking. The Internet Explorer security features will then become apparent. *Never* make purchases on a site that's not secure.

2. Look at the 'http://' part of the web address. If the site is secure it becomes https://. The 's' after the http shows that it is secure (A in Fig. 23).

3. On some sites the word secure may also be present somewhere within the web address e.g. https://www.secure or https://secure (B).

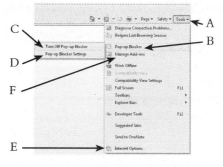

Fig. 21

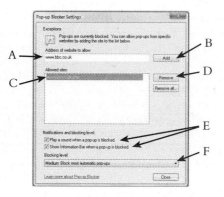

Fig. 22

4. A padlock (C) next to the web address at the top of Internet Explorer is evidence of a secure site.

5. Click on the padlock and the **Website Identification** box opens. Click on **View certificates** (D) to check on the security certificate of the website. Certificates are used to ensure that a secure site's identity is authentic, ensures privacy and that information is encrypted.

6. Look to see that the certificate is up to date (F) and the authority it was issued by (E).

7. Click **OK** to close the certificate.

Section 15:
Internet Security

The settings on **Internet Options** enable you to restrict sites and to create a list of web addresses of sites that you trust and also adjust the settings to increase the level of security should events require it.

Setting Security on Internet Explorer

1. Open **Internet Explorer**.

2. Click on **Tools**, click on **Internet Options** (E in Fig. 21).

3. Click on the **Security** tab (A in Fig. 24).

4. At the top of the tab under **Select a zone to view or change security settings** are icons of various zones (B), as listed below:

Internet

1. Click on the **Internet** icon (C) in **Select a zone to view or change security settings**.

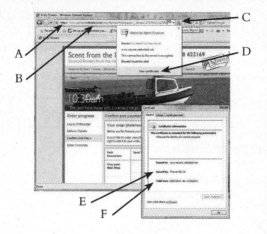

Fig. 23

2. Use the slider (D) to select a security level (medium-high is good).

3. Place a tick in the check box by **Enable Protected Mode** (E).

4. Click on **Apply** and then **OK** (F).

Trusted Sites

1. Click on the **Trusted Sites** icon (A in Fig. 25).

2. Using the slider (B) select a security level – this can be lower than that of general Internet sites.

3. Click to place a tick in the check box for **Enable Protected Mode** (C).

4. Click on the **Sites** button (D). The **Trusted sites** box opens.

5. To add a site that you trust, type or copy and paste its website address in the address bar (E).

6. Click on the **Add** button (F).

7. Remove a website by highlighting it and clicking on **Remove** (G).

8. Click on **Close** (H) to return to Internet Options.

Restricted Sites

1. Click on the **Restricted Sites** icon.
2. Select a security level – preferably **High**.
3. Click to place a tick in the check box for **Enable Protected Mode**.
4. Click on the **Sites** button.
5. Enter the website address into the address bar.
6. Click on **Add**.
7. To remove a site, highlight it and click on **Remove**.

Section 16:
Managing and Removing Add-ons

Add-ons are extra programs that can be added to Internet Explorer to increase its versatility – such as extra search toolbars. Some are created by Microsoft but others are provided by a variety of companies and you may start to find them irritating or they may even cause Internet Explorer to slow down. You can, if you wish, disable a toolbar. If you later wish to use it again, it can be turned back on.

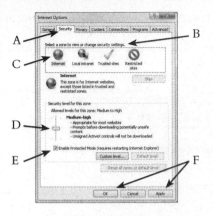

Fig. 24

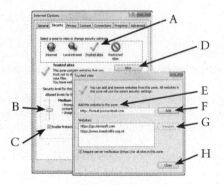

Fig. 25

1. In Internet Explorer click on **Tools** and then **Manage Add-ons** (F in Fig. 21).
2. Select a type of add-on in the **Add-on Types** column (A in Fig. 26).
3. Click on the add-on you wish to manage (B).
4. Click on **Disable** (C) (or **Enable** if it is already disabled and you now wish to use it).
5. Click on **Close** (D).

Section 17:
Blocking Information-gathering Using InPrivate Filtering

InPrivate Filtering filters out some of the information-gathering programs which are used by content providers to track your use of websites. Many web pages contain advertisements from third parties. By tracking your visits over a period of time, providers can build up a profile of your viewing activities, which can be used for various promotion and sales purposes. **InPrivate Filtering** enables you to keep some control over the information the providers manage to glean. However, if you use it you sometimes may not be able to download all the content of a web page. Fortunately, **InPrivate Filtering** is very easy to disengage from the filter.

Turning on InPrivate Filtering
1. On Internet Explorer 8 click on the **Safety** button (A in Fig. 27).

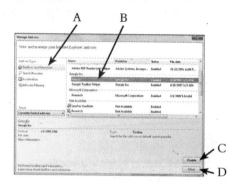

Fig. 26

Fig. 27

2. Click to place a tick (if not already there) by **InPrivate Filtering** (B).

3. On the first time of use you will be asked to select either **Block for me** or **Let me choose which providers receive my information**.

4. On subsequent use you can open the **InPrivate Filtering settings** dialog box (Fig. 28) by clicking on the **Safety** button and selecting **InPrivate Filtering Settings** (C in Fig. 27).

5. By clicking the radio button (A in Fig. 28) next to **Choose content to block or allow** you can highlight a content provider (B) and then to click on the **Allow** or **Block** buttons (C).

6. Click **OK**.

Turning off InPrivate Filtering

If the content of a web page is blocked and you wish to view it then:

1. Click the downward-pointing arrow (A in Fig. 29) by the **InPrivate Filtering** icon.

2. Click on **Off** (B) and **InPrivate Filtering** will be turned off and the web page content will then download.

3. This menu can be used to quickly turn on or off the filter, to change the settings, or to automatically block a site.

Extra: the InPrivate Filter is turned off automatically when you close Internet Explorer, so you will need to turn it on again next time it is opened.

InPrivate Filtering Options

1. Open **Internet Explorer**.

2. Click on **Tools**, then click on **Internet Options**.

3. Click on the **Privacy** tab (A in Fig. 30) of **Internet Options**.

4. At the bottom of the dialog box, under **InPrivate**, make sure that there is **no** tick in the check box next to **Do not**

Fig. 28

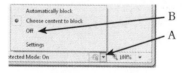

Fig. 29

collect data for use by InPrivate Filtering (C). This
will prevent websites from sharing your web visit details
with other websites.
5. Click on **Apply** and then **OK** (D).

Section 18:
Managing Cookies

Cookies are temporary Internet files that are stored on your computer. They are generated when you visit a website and contain very basic information about your visit and allow the website to send information to you; some sites may share this information with others. If you wish to maintain a higher level of privacy, cookies can be controlled or blocked. Blocking all cookies, however, may mean that you will not be able to access some websites. A **Medium High** setting will block cookies from those sites that do not have a good privacy policy for visitors.

Controlling Cookies

1. Open Internet Explorer. Click on **Tools** on the menu bar and from the drop-down menu select **Internet Options**.
2. Click on the **Privacy** (A In Fig. 30) tab.
3. Select a level by moving the slider (B) either up or down.
4. Click on **Apply** and then **OK** (C).

To Remove Cookies

1. Open Internet Explorer. Click on **Tools** on the menu bar.
2. Click **Internet Options**, and then click on the **General** tab (A in Fig. 31).
3. Under **Browsing history**, click on **Delete** (B).
4. This also gets rid of other temporary Internet files. (To view them first, click on **Settings** (C) and then **View Files**.)
5. Use the spin buttons under **History** to choose how many days Internet Explorer saves the list of websites that you have visited.

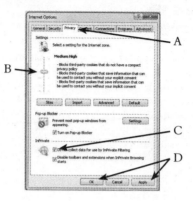

Fig. 30

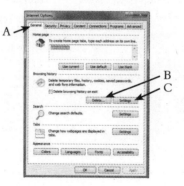

Fig. 31

Section 19:
Parental Controls

It's generally considered to be unwise to allow a child unlimited access to a computer or the Internet. However, even the most diligent parent cannot always be present to monitor their child's computer activities. The parental controls on Windows 7 enable you to specify the length of time spent on the computer, what games are played and what programs can be used. The different levels can be adjusted according to the child's age.

1. Click on Start and Control Panel and in category view, under User Accounts and Family Safety click on **Set up parental controls for any user**.
2. Click once on the child's user name and a new window will open.
3. Under Parental Controls, click on the option button next to **On, enforce current settings** (A in Fig. 32).
4. This activates the Windows Settings (B), which you can use to set time limits on computer usage (C), to control games played (D) and to allow or block programs (E).
5. As you chose various settings they will be listed under the child's user name on the right of the window (F).

Setting Time Limits
1. Click on **Time limits** (C) under Windows Settings. A new window opens with a 24-hour chart: white squares are hours when computer time is **Allowed**; the coloured areas represent areas when access is denied or **Blocked**.

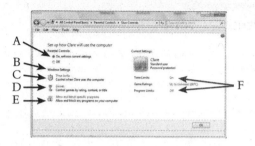

Fig. 32

2. Click on individual squares or click and drag across a section to block a time period, thus creating a timetable of when the computer can be used by a child.

3. Click **OK** to save the settings.

Game Restriction

Internet games can be blocked or the content, title and rating of any game that is allowed can be controlled. When you set ratings these will also apply to games already installed on your computer.

1. Click on **Games** (D) under Window Settings and a new window opens.

2. Click the relevant option button by **Yes** or **No** (A in Fig. 33) to determine whether the child is allowed to play computer games.

3. To filter the type of games accessed, click on **Set game ratings**.

4. A new window opens. Click on the option button by **Block games with no rating** (B).

5. Click in the option buttons to select the rating level allowed (C). Scroll down the page to select check boxes to further block content.

6. Click **OK**. You are returned to the Games Control window.

7. To block or allow games already installed on your computer click on **Block or Allow specific games** (D) and then on option buttons to allow or block specific games, then **OK**.

Allow or Block Specific Programs a child is allowed to use

1. Under Windows Settings click on **Allow and block specific programs** (E in Fig. 32).

2. Click to select either **Can use all programs** or **Only use the programs I allow**. If you chose the latter a list of computer programs will be downloaded. Click to place a tick in the check boxes of allowed programs.

3. Click **OK**.

Restricting Internet Access

To prevent children coming into contact with web material that is unsuitable, harmful and frightening you can adjust Internet Explorer's Content Advisor settings to control or restrict the download of any inappropriate material. This affects all users but the Content Advisor can be turned off at any time by using the password that you will have created.

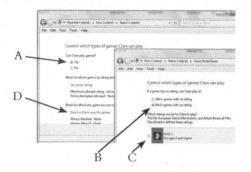

Fig. 33

1. Type **Internet Options** in the Start menu Search box. Click on it to open the **Internet Properties** box. Click on the **Content** tab (A in Fig. 34).

2. Under Content Advisor click on **Enable** (B) <u>and on the first time of using</u>, **Contents Advisor** (see Fig. 35) opens.

3. Click on the **Ratings** tab (A), select a category (D) and drag the slider (E) to the level of restriction you wish to apply. Repeat for the other categories.

4. Click on the **Approved Sites** tab (B) and enter the web addresses of those sites you wish to allow.

5. Click on the **General** tab (C). Click the check box by **Supervisor can type a password to allow users to view restricted content**.

6. Click on **Create password**. Create a password so that only you and not the child can alter the settings you have selected. This becomes **Change password** after a password has been created.

7. To change the settings, click on the Content tab. Under Content Advisor, click on either **Disable** to turn off or **Settings** to alter. You will need your supervisor password.

Family Safety

Family Safety is a program available free from Windows Live Essentials and can be used to enhance the existing parental controls. See Chapter Two, Section 13 on how to access Windows Live Essentials.

Further Parental Controls

For further parental controls there are a variety of software programs available. You may wish to check out:

Net Nanny: www.net-nanny-software.com
Cyber Sitter: www.cybersitter.com
Software 4 Parents: www.software4parents.com
This is not an endorsement of any of the above products.

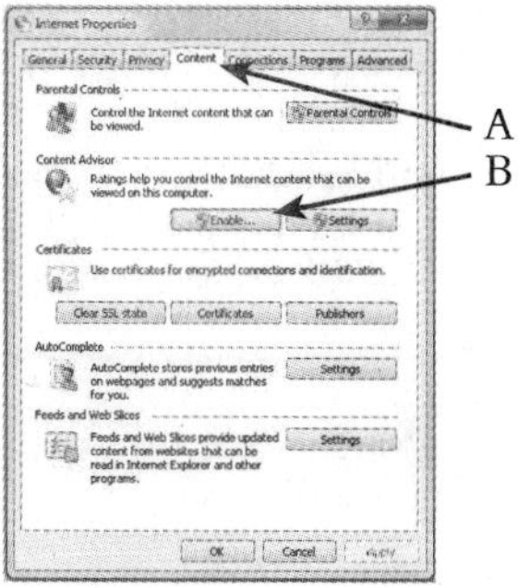
Internet Properties
General
Security
Privacy
Content
Connections
Programs
Advanced
Parental Controls
Control the Internet content that can be viewed.
Parental Controls
Content Advisor
Ratings help you control the Internet content that can be viewed on this computer.
Enable...
Settings
Certificates
Use certificates for encrypted connections and identification.
Clear SSL state
Certificates
Publishers
AutoComplete
AutoComplete stores previous entries on webpages and suggests matches for you.
Settings
Feeds and Web Slices
Feeds and Web Slices provide updated content from websites that can be read in Internet Explorer and other programs.
Settings
OK
Cancel
Apply
A
B

Fig. 34

A
B
C
D
Ratings
Approved Sites
General
Advanced
Select a category to view the rating levels:
ICRA3
Content that sets a bad example for young children
Depiction of alcohol use
Depiction of drug use
Depiction of gambling
Adjust the slider to specify what users are allowed to see:
E
None
Description
No content that creates feelings of fear, intimidation, etc. in any context
To view the Internet page for this rating service, click More Info.
More Info
OK
Cancel
Apply

Fig. 35

Chapter Eleven:
The Internet

Today the Internet has become an integral part of everyday life, allowing us to do many things: shop online, send emails, search for information, read the news, access newsgroups, films, television stations, listen to the radio and download music. If you live in the UK the Internet is available for public use on the computers in the local library. It's a good place to gain your first experience of the internet and there's usually someone around who is willing to share their expertise.

Section 1:
Getting Connected to the Internet at Home

Internet Service Providers

You will need to sign up to an account with an Internet Service Provider (ISP). Make sure that the ISP you choose will be delivering the services you want. Ask for an information pack and check if they have a telephone helpline and how much it costs – many offer free helplines, others charge by the minute. The type of connection that you have may well be dictated by where you live; there are three options – Broadband, Wireless and Dial-up.

A broadband connection is faster at downloading material from the Internet and you can use the telephone at the same time. If you live in an area where broadband is unavailable then you will be offered a dial-up connection – this uses the normal telephone connection to access the Internet and has to be used separately to the telephone.

Fig. 1

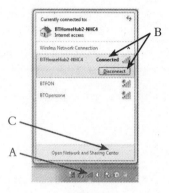

Fig. 2

Getting Connected

Once you have set up an account, the ISP will give you an initial user name and password and you can get started by using the Windows 7 **Connect to the Internet Wizard**.

1. Click the Internet Connection icon (A in Fig. 1) on the taskbar to open a box which shows the **Connected** and **Disconnect** buttons (B). Click on **Open Network and Sharing Center** (C).

2. Click **Set up a new connection or network** (A in Fig. 2).

3. In the box that opens click on **Connect to the Internet** (B) and then click **Next**.

4. Click the option that you are going to use to connect to the Internet: Wireless, Broadband or Dial-up (A in Fig. 3). If your option is not listed click to place a tick in the check box by **Show connection options that this computer is not set up to use** (B).

5. Enter the information that the ISP has given you into the boxes (A in Fig. 4).

6. Select the check box by **Remember this password** (B) if you don't want to have to type it in whenever you go online. Select or clear the check box by **Show characters** (C).

7. Type in a name in the text box by **Connection name** (D).

8. Add or remove a tick in the check box by **Allow other people to use this connection** (E).

9. Click **Connect** (F).

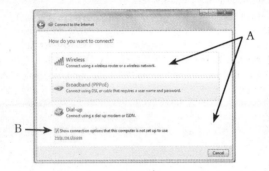

Fig. 3

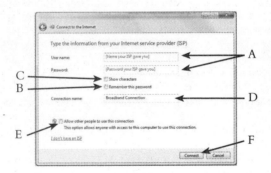

Fig. 4

To Connect to and Disconnect from the Internet

1. Click on the Network Connection icon on the taskbar.
2. Click on the connection name that you are using.
3. Click on the **Connect** or **Disconnect** button that appears and whichever is appropriate.

Safety and Security on the Internet

Read Chapter Ten for details about staying safe and secure when using the Internet, email and online shopping. Chapter Ten also includes Internet parental controls.

Section 2:
An Overview of Internet Explorer

Windows 7 comes with **Internet Explorer 8** – the latest Microsoft web browser. It has the familiar layout of previous editions but IE8 starts and loads more quickly, has increased security features and other tools that enable smooth and efficient browsing of the web. See also Chapter Ten for details on Internet security.

Open Internet Explorer 8

Click on the Internet Explorer icon on the taskbar or click on the Start menu and select Internet Explorer.

The Internet Explorer Window

1. Type in a web address in the **Address Bar** (B in Fig. 5).
2. The **Status Bar** (L) reminds you if the **Internet Protected Mode** is on or off, and holds the **Zoom** and **InPrivate Filtering** tools.

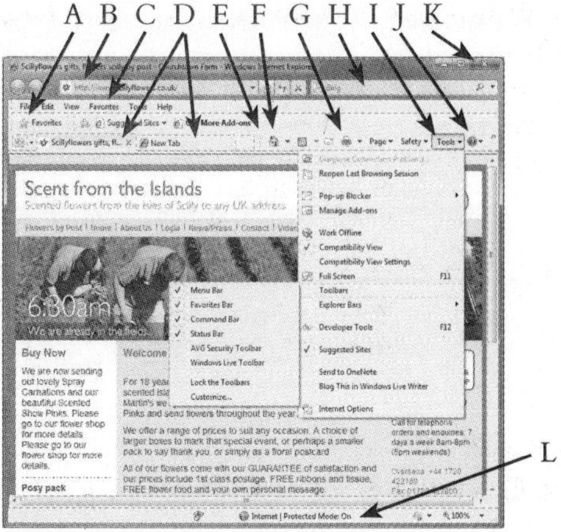

Fig. 5

3. The **Instant search** (H) text box enables you to search the Internet.

4. The **Tabs** (D) allow you to have different web pages open at the same time.

5. Use the **Favorites** button (A) to save and access your favourite web addresses.

6. Click on the **Help** (J) button to find out more about using Internet Explorer.

7. Click on the **Home** (F) button to take you back to your Home page.

8. To print a web page, click on the **Print** button (G).

9. The **menu bar** (C) carries many Internet Explorer tools to give you versatility in using the web.

10. Click on the **Tools** button (I) and a drop-down menu gives you access to turning on and off the different **Toolbars** and to **Full Screen** which expands Internet Explorer to cover the whole screen.

11. The 'handles' (E) on the toolbars allow you to move the toolbar sideways to see any hidden tools.

12. If you click on **Lock the Toolbars** on the Tools drop-down sub-menu, the toolbar handle disappears, you cannot move the toolbars and the tools remain in position. To see the hidden tools click on the two sideways-pointing arrows.

13. To close **Internet Explorer 8** click on the **Close** (K) button.

Section 3:
Navigating Internet Explorer

As you browse the web and move from site to site and page to page, you may find that you wish to go back to a previous page or forward to another. A page may also not download correctly or you may wish to stop it downloading. Older websites may also not download properly and need to be made compatible.

Back, Forward and Home

1. Use the **Back** button (A in Fig. 6) to go back one page.

2. Use the **Forward** button (B) to move forward one page.

3. Click on the down arrow (C) by the Back/Forward buttons to see a list of recent sites (D).

4. Click on a name to revisit a site.

5. Click on **History** (E) to see more previously visited sites.

6. To return to your Home page, click on the **Home** (D in Fig.7) button.

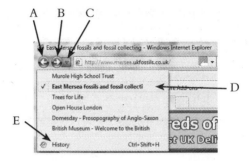

Fig. 6

Fig. 7

Stop and Refresh a Page

1. To stop a page downloading, click on the **Stop** button (C in Fig. 7) by the address bar.
2. To refresh a page click on the **Refresh** button (B).

Compatibility of Older Websites

1. If the downloaded page does not appear to be working correctly, try clicking on the compatibility button (A in Fig. 7). It may be an older site.

2. Once activated, the button remains depressed and a message appears on the screen informing you that the website is running in compatibility view (E).

3. If the web page does not correct itself then there is most likely a problem within its site design.

Section 4:
Your Explorer Home Page

The first time you use Windows 7 and IE8 you may be connected to the Microsoft Home page. However, you can select any website to be your Home page or you can have a collection of them. When you connect to the Internet and then start Internet Explorer it will immediately download the page that you have chosen for your Home page. If for some reason you no longer wish to keep a web page as a Home page it can be removed from your collection.

1. Open up Internet Explorer 8, and connect to the Internet.

2. Open the web page you have chosen for your Home page.

3. Click on the downward-pointing arrow by the Home icon (A in Fig. 8).

4. Click on **Add or Change Home Page** (B).

Fig. 8

5. Use the options buttons (C) on the box to select the web page as the only Home page or to add to a collection of Home page tabs.

6. Click on **Yes** (D) to save the option that you have chosen.

*Note: to remove a page as a Home page, repeat steps 1–3 above and then click on **Remove** (B) on the drop-down menu. A sub-menu opens listing your Home pages. Click on the page you wish to remove.*

Section 5:
The Layout of a Web Page

Each website has a Home page which carries a variety of links leading a visitor through its many pages. Links can exist as pictures, text, or graphics. Move the mouse pointer onto a link and the arrow turns into a small hand with a pointed finger – click on the link and a new page will download. A website may also have a **contents list** – either the top of the page or at the side. If the site is a large one there may also be a **site map**.

Links

1. On the site shown in Fig. 9 the **contents list** (A) is shown at the top of the page.
2. The **Home** (B) link on the contents list returns you to the site's Home page.
3. The contents lists often have drop-down menus (C) which have further links.
4. **Text links** (D) are sometimes in blue, but can be different colours.
5. **Picture links** (E) will download another page when clicked.
6. Many large websites have their own **site search** (F) facility to help you find information contained within their own website and sometimes across the web.

Email a Web Link

1. Have your web page open and right-click the link that you wish to email.
2. On the drop-down menu, click on **E-mail with Windows Live**.
3. Sign in to **Windows Live**.
4. Enter the email address of the recipient. The subject is entered automatically.
5. Click on **Send**.

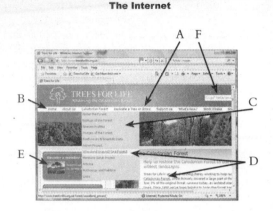

Fig. 9

Section 6:
Browsing the Web and Web Addresses

Every website has its own unique web address (or URL) and each page within a website carries the main website address plus its own page identification. The web address must be accurately entered into the Internet Explorer address bar.

The dots, colons and forward slashes of a web address are very important and must not be left out: for example, http://www.britishmuseum.org/

The web address for the 'What's on' page at the British Museum is: http://www.britishmuseum.org/whats_on.aspx

There are no spaces in the address.

There's no need for you to type the 'www' part of the web address as Internet Explorer enters this automatically. It also comes with AutoComplete which remembers previously entered web addresses and tries to match addresses as you type. They are listed in a drop-down menu.

Type a New Web Address

1. Click in the address bar (A in Fig. 10). Delete any current web address by using the backspace or delete key.
2. Type in the web address. Do not type in http//:www – this will be added automatically.
3. Click the Go button (B) or press **Enter** on the keyboard and the page will download.

Type in a Previously Visited Web Address

1. Click in the address bar (A). Delete any current web address.
2. Start to type in the web address.
3. As you type the first few letters (C), AutoComplete tries to find matches from previously visited sites (D).
4. Check on the drop-down list whether the website you are seeking is listed.
5. If it is, click on it and the web page will download.
6. The History list will also show web *page* addresses (E) previously visited from *within* the website, so you can even go straight to an individual page.

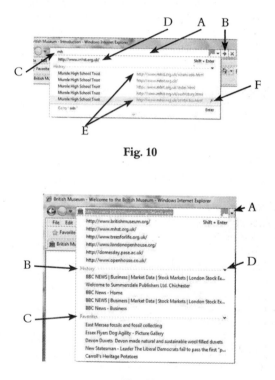

Fig. 10

Fig. 11

The Address Bar and Recent, History and Favorites Lists

1. Click on the address bar down arrow (A in Fig. 11) and look on the drop-down list to find previously visited sites and sites in the **History** (B) or **Favorites** (C) lists.
2. Click on the arrows to expand the lists (D).
3. Click on any address in the list to download the website.

Delete a Web Address from the Lists

1. Move the cursor down over the web addresses in the address bar lists.
2. As you do so a red cross (F in Fig. 10) will appear to the right of the address.
3. Click on the red cross and the address is deleted from the lists.

Section 7:
Browsing the Web Using Tabs

Tabs allow you to open a number of pages from a single website and also other websites, all within one Internet Explorer window.

1. The tabs of pages from one website are grouped together, in one colour (A in Fig. 12). The tabs of a different website will be in a different colour – making it easy to keep track.
2. Click on a new tab and it becomes **New Tab** (B) with a number of 'getting started' links (C) on the page. Click to find out more or to reopen closed tabs.

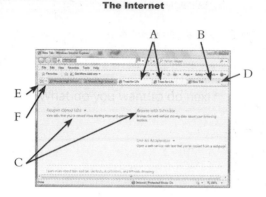

Fig. 12

Using Tabs within a Website or Open in a New Window

It's easy to open different pages of a web site on different tabs. If you wish you can also open a page in a new window.
1. Right-click on a link on the currently opened web site.
2. Click on **Open in New Tab** on the drop-down menu.
3. The web page connected to the link will open in a new tab.
4. Click on the tab to view the page.
5. To open the page in a **New Window**, click on **Open in New Window**.

Close a Tab

1. Click on the tab and move the pointer onto the cross (D in Fig. 12) on the tab.
2. Click on it to close the tab.

Close a Group of Tabs

1. Right-click on one of the tabs in the group.
2. From the drop-down menu click on **Close this Tab Group**.

Quick Tabs Button

The **Quick Tabs** button (E in Fig. 12) is displayed when more than one tab is being used. This allows you to quickly see what pages or sites you currently have open.

1. To view a list of open tabs click on the *arrow* (F) by **Quick Tabs**.
2. Click on the Quick Tabs *button* (E) and the open tabs are shown as thumbnail images.

Section 8:
Browsing the Web Privately

If you are using a computer away from home and it is running Windows 7 you can maintain your privacy with the **InPrivate Browsing** feature. This means that the computer does not keep track of your browsing history, cookies, passwords or user names thus preventing others who also have access to the computer knowing which web pages you have viewed.

1. Click on a **New Tab** (A in Fig. 13).
2. Click on the link **Open an InPrivate Browsing window** (B).
3. A new window opens with the **InPrivate** indicator (C) in the address bar.

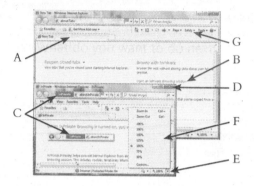

Fig. 13

4. While you view web pages within this window the indicator will remain and your privacy will be maintained.

5. To close **InPrivate Browsing** click on the **Close** button (D) on the window.

If you are browsing without InPrivate, you can still delete your browsing history, temporary internet files and cookies manually – see Chapter Ten, Section 15.

Section 9:
Web Page Zooming and Larger Text

The Zoom tool allows you to increase or decrease the size of everything on the web page. It is located at the bottom right of the Internet Explorer window.

1. Click on the downward-pointing arrow (E in Fig. 13).
2. From the **Zoom** menu (F) choose the zoom level that you wish to use.
3. To increase or decrease the size of text on a web page, click on **Page** (G) on the toolbar.
4. On the drop-down menu, click on **Text Size** and from the sub-menu click on the size that you wish to use.

Section 10:
Pop-ups

Read Chapter Ten, Section 10 about managing pop-ups and security. Pop-ups can be harmless advertising mini windows that appear when you download a web page. But to make sure that you do not inadvertently download a virus via a malicious pop-up you should ensure that the pop-up blocker is on. To check that it is working effectively you could try out pop-up testing sites. If the pop-up blocker is working correctly, a bar will appear across the top of Internet Explorer (A in Fig. 14). Right-click the bar and a menu (B) and sub-menu allows you to choose to temporarily download the pop-up or if it is a trusted site to always allow pop-ups. You can also turn the pop-up blocker on or off.

Some sites to try out this technique on are popupcheck. com and popuptest.com

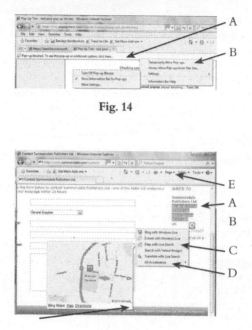

Fig. 14

Fig. 15

Section 11:
Using Accelerators to Browse the Web

Accelerators are a new built-in feature of Internet Explorer 8. They enable you to search the Internet more quickly, easily and efficiently and to get maps, translations and definitions. There are many more accelerators available to download and these can be added to Internet Explorer if you wish.

1. Open up a web page and highlight a piece of text that contains information that you wish to research further. We have highlighted an address (A in Fig. 15).

2. Click the blue Accelerator icon (B) that appears when you highlight the text.

3. Point to an accelerator (C) or All Accelerators (D).

4. Move your pointer over the list of accelerators and some will display appropriate search results in a small window. Click anywhere on the small window to open in a new full size Internet Explorer tab.

5. Alternatively, click on any accelerator in the list to view search results in a new tab.

Get More Accelerators

1. Click on the **Page** button (E) on the command bar.

2. Click on **All Accelerators** from the drop-down menu. Click **Find More Accelerators**.

3. This takes you to the Internet Explorer 8 website where you can click on the accelerator that you wish to add.

Manage Accelerators

Accelerators are add-ons and can be very useful. Sometimes, though, you may just end up with too many and want to remove or disable them. This is covered fully in Chapter Ten on Security. To get to the Manage Add-ons window:

1. Click on the **Page** button on the command bar.

2. Click on **All Accelerators** from the drop-down menu. Click on **Manage Accelerators**.

3. Use this window to remove, disable or set as default any of the accelerators you have added on:

Section 12:
The Favorites Bar

Use the Favorites Center and Bar to keep a record of sites that you have visited and would like to use again. You can then return to a website by clicking on it in the Favorites list or on the Bar. You can also create and organise folders within Favorites to help you stay organised.

Open Favorites
Click on the **Favorites** button (A in Fig. 16) on the toolbar.
Pin Favorites
1. Click on the **Pin** arrow (B) to keep the Favorites Center and List open while you are using Internet Explorer.

2. Click on the **Close** button that replaces the Pin arrow to close the list.

Add to Favorites
1. With a web page open, click on the **Add to Favorites** button (C in Fig. 16) on the Favorites bar.

2. In the **Add a Favorite** text box (D), the name of the web page will be listed.

3. To add your own title, click in the text box and type in a name.

4. Click on the **Add** button (E) and the web page address will be saved.

5. To save the web address in a folder, click on the downward pointing arrow (F) by **Create in:** select a folder and click **Add**.

6. To create a new folder, click on the **New Folder** button (G).

7. In the **Create a Folder** box, give the folder a name and click **Create**.

Add a Web Page to the Favorites Bar

1. Have the web page open, then click on **Favorites** (A in Fig. 17) then **Add to Favorites Bar** (B).

2. The name of the website appears as a button (C) on the Favorites Bar.

3. To revisit the website, just click on the button.

Add a Group of Tabs to Favorites

1. While you have your group of tabs open, click on the **Favorites** button.

2. Click on the down arrow (D in Fig. 17) by **Add to Favorites** and then on the drop-down menu click on **Add Current Tabs to Favorites** (E).

Revisit a Favorite

1. Click on the **Favorites** button. Click on a web address (F in Fig. 17) and the web page will download onto the current tab.

2. To open a Favorite in a new tab, click on the blue arrow on the right side of the address.

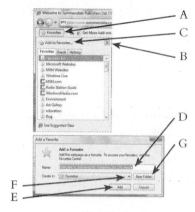

Fig. 16

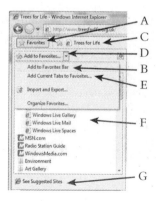

Fig. 17

3. To open a group of tabs, click the folder that holds the web addresses and click on the blue arrow on the right side of the folder.

4. To revisit a website you've looked at a while ago, click on **Favorites**, then on the **History** tab (A in Fig. 18), click on a folder to open a list of web addresses.

5. To sort the **History** tab click the down arrow (B) under History and a list allows you to view your recent visits by Date, Site, Most Visited, etc. (C).

6. Click to open a folder and then on the website that you wish to revisit.

Note: see Chapter Ten on security for how to delete your history list.

Suggested Sites
Suggested Sites is a new and free online service from Microsoft.

1. Open a website that is of interest to you.

2. Click on **Suggested Sites** (G in Fig. 17) on Favorites and sites similar to the one you are viewing are listed. Click on one to view.

Section 13:
Organising Favorites

Your favourite web addresses can be organised and managed by creating new folders, renaming, moving and deleting them. Individual web addresses can also be deleted from the Favorites list. Click on the **Favorites** button to open. Click on the down arrow by **Add to Favorites**. Click on **Organize Favorites**.

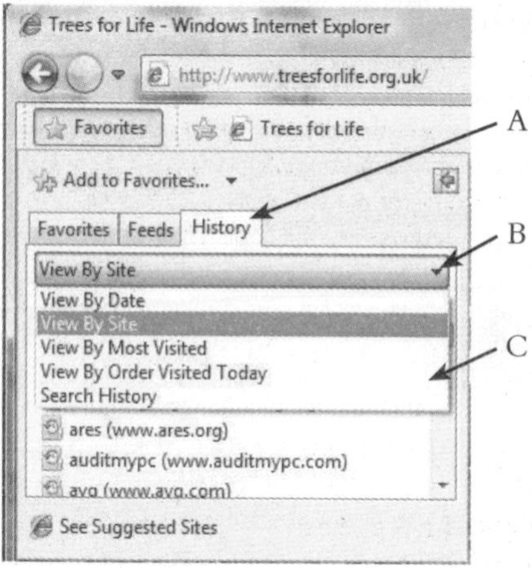

Fig. 18

Renaming and Deleting

1. Highlight a folder (A in Fig. 19) and click on **Rename** (B).
2. Type in a new name. Press Enter on the keyboard and the name is saved.
3. Highlight the item to be deleted and click on the **Delete** button (C).
4. On the message box, click **Yes** to dump or **No** to keep.

Create a New Folder

1. Click on **New Folder** (D in Fig. 19).
2. A **New Folder** opens in **Organize Favorites**.
3. Type in a name. Press **Enter** on the keyboard to save.

Moving a Folder or Favorite

1. Locate the the folder or favorite to be moved, and click to highlight it.
2. Click on **Move** (E in Fig. 19).
3. In **Browse for Folder** click on the folder that you want to move the file into.
4. Click on **OK**.

Section 14:
Searching the Web

There is an enormous amount of information on the Internet and to search for a specific topic you will need to use the web search tools to sift through what is available. There is a search facility on Internet Explorer and you can add other search engines such as Google, Yahoo, Wikipedia, Ask Jeeves, Altavista and Bing. These search engines comb the Internet pages for compatibility with certain keywords that you provide in a search bar.

Using Internet Explorer Search Bar

1. Type in your search words into the Internet Explorer search bar (A in Fig. 20). As you type a list appears with suggested page links.
2. Carry on typing if none of them match what you are looking for. Click on the **Search** button (B).
3. Internet Explorer lists links to pages that appear to match your search.
4. Click to open or continue to use the search bar to refine your search.

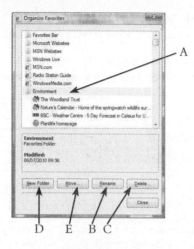

Fig. 19

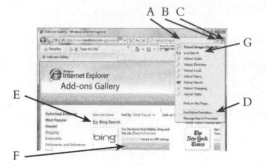

Fig. 20

5. If you are unsuccessful, try one of the other search engines.

To Find More Search Engines

1. Click on the down arrow (C in Fig. 20) by the search bar.
2. On the drop-down menu click on **Find More Providers** (D).
3. This connects you to Internet Explorer 8 Add-ons Gallery website (E).
4. Choose a search engine.
5. Click on **Add to Internet Explorer** (F) and the search engine is added to the Search drop-down list (G).

Searching Using Keywords

Use keywords when making a search. Very often a single word will find what you want. When using more than one word, type them in descending order of importance. Those sites that have the best matches to the keywords are always listed first. When you search using a specific phrase place it in quotation marks, e.g. 'I had a dream'.

Finding Text on a Page

1. Click the search bar arrow (A in Fig. 21).
2. Click **Find on this page** (B) and the **Find** toolbar is displayed (C).
3. Click the **Options** button (D) to highlight in yellow (E) the words you are searching for.
4. You can also make your search more specific. Click the **Options** arrow and select from the list either **Match Whole Word Only** or **Match Case**.

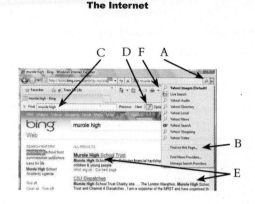

Fig. 21

5. Type the words you are searching for in the Find text box (C).

6. As you type the words are highlighted in the text.

7. To close the toolbar, click on the **Close** button.

Section 15:
Printing a Web Page

Before you print a web page it's a good idea to first view it on **Print Preview**. This will show you how the web page will look on your printed page rather than how it looks on the screen; you can also see how many pages you may be printing.

Internet Explorer Print Preview and Printing

1. Click on the down arrow by the **Print** button (F in Fig. 21).

2. Click on **Print Preview** on the drop-down list.

3. The **Print Preview window** opens.

4. Allow your pointer to hover on each button on the Print Preview bar and an identification label will appear. These buttons enable you to orientate your printing, access page set-up, shrink a page to fit your printer and view more than one page at a time. Experiment with each to see how they work.

5. When you are ready to print click on the **Print** button.

6. The **Print** dialog box opens.

7. Click on the **General** tab.

8. Click on the name of the printer to be used, the number of copies to be printed, and the page range. Click **Print**.

*Note: if you decide to by pass Print Preview and print straight from Internet Explorer, click on the **Print** button on the command bar, and from the drop-down list click on **Print**.*

Chapter Twelve:
Windows Live Mail

The email program **Windows Live Mail** replaces Windows Mail and Outlook Express from the previous Windows versions. It does not come already installed as part of Windows 7 but it is available as a *free download* from **Windows Live Essentials** with Hotmail as the Email Service Provider. For more on Internet Service Providers see Chapter Eleven, Section 1.

Section 1:
Getting Started and Creating an Account

Download Windows Live Mail and Create a Free Hotmail Account

1. Connect to the Internet, click on the **Start** menu button and then on **Getting Started** (A in Fig. 1).
2. Click on **Get Windows Live Essentials** (B) which will take you straight to the Microsoft website.
3. Click on the **Download now** button to download all the Live Essential software. If you wish to download and install just the email package, click on Mail and then on **Download now**. (You may need to remove ticks from check boxes by programs that you do not wish to download.)
4. Follow the screen prompts as they appear.
5. When you reach the **Welcome to Windows Live!** window (A in Fig. 2) click on the **Sign up** link (B). This

will enable you to create your Window Live ID (C) which will also form your email address (multiple email accounts are available with Hotmail). You can also use it to access any of the Windows Live Essentials.

6. Enter all the information required.

7. If an email address has already been used you can click on the **Check availability** button (D) for similar alternatives.

8. When you have finished entering the necessary information you will need to click **I accept** to agree to the Microsoft terms and conditions of use.

*Note: if you do not want to sign in during the downloading process it can be done later by clicking on the **Sign in** button on the email window (C in Fig. 3).*

Open Windows Live Mail and Download Folders

1. Click on the **Start** button, then **All Programs**.

2. Look for the folder **Windows Live** (C in Fig. 1). Click to open.

3. Click on **Windows Live Mail** (D in Fig. 1).

4. On the first time of using, click on your account name (A in Fig. 3) and then click on the **Download** button (B) to download the folders which will sit in the Folders list under your account name.

5. Pin the **Mail** icon to the taskbar and Start menu for quicker access (see Chapter Two, Section 9).

Fig. 1

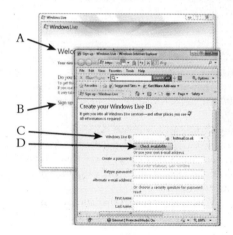

Fig. 2

Add another Email Account from Hotmail or another ISP

If you already have an email account with a different Internet Service Provider, or decide to get another one in the future, it can be added to the Windows Live Mail window using the email wizard. You will need the information provided by your email server. If you wish you can also use the wizard to add another Hotmail account.

1. Open Windows Live Mail.
2. In the Folders list click on **Add e-mail account** (A in Fig. 4). This will open the email wizard which will configure the email account for you. (If you wish to open another Hotmail account, click on the link **Get a free email account**.)
3. Type in your email address, password and display name (B).
4. Place a tick in the check box **Remember password** (C).
5. Clear the check box by **Manually configure server settings for e-mail account** (D) in order for the wizard to configure automatically.
6. Click **Next** (E).
7. Click **Finish**.

Making Windows Live Mail your Default Email Program

When you set Windows Live Mail as your default email it will automatically appear when you click on an email link on a web page or on an email button on an Explorer window.

1. Click on the Start button, on **All Programs** and then on **Default Programs**.
2. Click on **Set your default programs** and a new window opens.

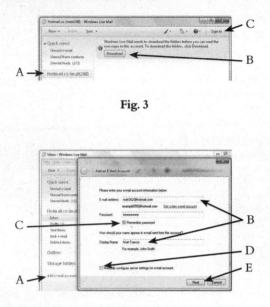

Fig. 3

Fig. 4

3. Under the list of programs on the left of the window locate and click on Windows Live Mail.
4. On the right of the window click on **Set this program as default**.
5. Click **OK**.

Note: if you have a different email program which you wish to use as a default use the same procedure.

Email Addresses

These contain a person's name, the Internet Service Provider's name, the type of organisation (co, org, ac or com) and (outside of America) a country's code, e.g. anybody@serviceprovider.co.uk. When you type an email address remember all the dots and do not include any spaces.

Section 2:
An Overview of the Windows Live Mail Window

The **Folders List** (A in Fig. 5) – shows the folders that hold your incoming and outgoing emails.

Quick views (C) – click on **Unread e-mail** to find unread emails, rather than searching your Inbox.

Account Name (M) – each account name has its own set of folders:
The **Inbox** is used to receive all emails.
Sent items lists all emails successfully sent.
When you delete an item it goes into **Deleted items**.
If you wish to compose a message but not send it immediately, it can be placed in the **Drafts** folder to send later.
The **Junk e-mail** folder is used to house spam and unwanted emails.

The **Outbox** (L) houses the outgoing mail of all accounts until you connect to the Internet to send them.

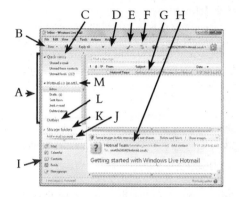

Fig. 5

Storage Folders (K) – are further folders available for storage of items you do not wish to include under your email account.

Programs, Toolbars and Panes:

The **Menu bar** (E) allows you to access various Mail commands.

The **Menu button** (F) opens various options including layout of the mail window.

The **Toolbar** (D) provides a variety of ways to work with your messages.

New (B) opens a new message window.

The **Programs area** (I) carries the programs contained in Windows Mail: Calendar, Contacts, Feeds and Newsgroups.

The **Message List** (G) shows the email messages.
The **Reading pane** (H) displays the contents of a selected message.
Add e-mail account (J) – this link accesses the email wizard to set up additional accounts.

Windows Live Mail Layout

There are a variety of ways to view Windows Live Mail – depending on the settings you select, your version may not look exactly the same as the screenshots in this book. Use the Menus button to change the layout.

1. Click on the **Menus button** (A in Fig. 6).
2. Click on **Layout** (B). The Layout box (C) opens.
3. Click an option button (D) to decide whether to place the reading pane to the bottom or to the right of the Message List.
4. Click on the other sections (E) and click on the check boxes or options buttons to decide how you wish Windows Live Mail to work for you.
5. When you have finished making your selections click on **Apply** (F) and then **OK** (G).

Section 3:
Reading, Writing and Sending an Email

Read an Email

1. In the Folders list, click on the black triangle to open your account if not already open and then click on **Inbox**. Or under **Quick Links** click on **Unread e-mail**.

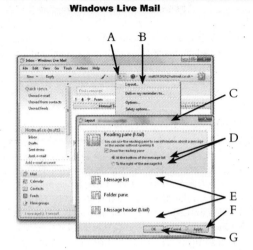

Fig. 6

2. The new messages received will be listed in bold text in the Message List.

3. Click on a message and its contents will be displayed in the reading pane, or you can double-click on the message and it will open in its own window.

Write and Send an Email Message

1. Click on the **New** button on the toolbar and a **New Message** window opens.

2. Click on **To:** and from your contacts list select a recipient (see Section 10). Then click **OK**. Or you can click in the **To:** text box (A in Fig. 7) and type in the email address.

3. Click in the **Subject:** text box (B) and give your message a short relevant title.

4. If you wish to send a copy to other recipients click on the link **Show Cc & Bcc** (D).

5. Enter an address in **Cc:** (Carbon copy) (J) if you wish other recipients to know who received the copy or **Bcc:** (Blind carbon copy) (K) if you do not.

6. Click in the message box (G) and type your message.

7. Click on the **Send** button (I). (If you are working offline, the message will be stored in the Outbox and be sent automatically the next time you go online.)

Section 4:
Formatting your Email

1. The **Formatting toolbar** (E in Fig. 7) enables you to format your message in a similar way to a Word document (see Chapter Six).

2. Rest your mouse cursor over a formatting tool to see its name label.

3. Use any of the tools to change the background colour, add an **emoticon** (H), highlight your text and check the spelling of your message.

4. A variety of additional background styles can be found by clicking on the down arrow by **Stationery** (F) and then on **More stationery**. In the **Select Stationery box** click on a style and then click **OK** to apply to the email.

5. To delete an emoticon from a message, right-click it and from the drop-down menu click **Undo** or **Delete**.

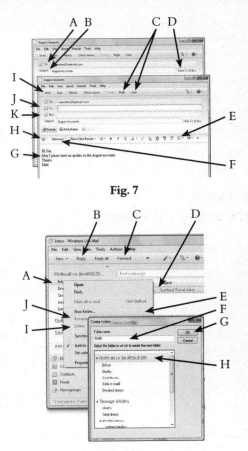

Fig. 7

Fig. 8

*Extra: design your own default email containing backgrounds, fonts and signatures by clicking on **Tools** on the menu bar on Windows Live Mail, then on **Options**, then the **Compose** tab. Choose fonts and stationery. Click on the **Help** icon on the Options box to learn more.*

Flag a Message or Give it a Priority

For an urgent or important message click on the **High** button (C in Fig. 7) to give your message high priority and a red flag; for an email of low priority click the **Low** button.

Section 5:
Replying to an Email

1. Click on the **Inbox** in the Folders list (A in Fig. 8). Highlight the message (D) and then click on the **Reply** button (B) on the toolbar.
2. The sender's email address and subject is automatically inserted into a new window, along with the original message.
3. Click in the message pane above the sender's message and type in your own text. Any of the sender's text not required can be highlighted and deleted.
4. Click on **Send**.

Forwarding an Email

1. Click on the email that you wish to forward and then click on the **Forward** button (C in Fig. 8).
2. A new window opens containing the forwarded message.
3. Click on **To:** to add the name(s) of the recipient(s).
4. Click on **Send**.

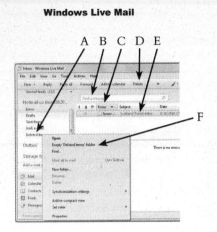

Fig. 9

Section 6:
Managing and Moving Messages

Windows Live Mail allows you to create folders and to manage and file your messages.

1. To create a folder, select the destination in the folders list, right-click on the mouse button and from the drop-down list click on **New Folder** (E in Fig. 8) and the **Create Folder** box is displayed.

2. Highlight the destination (H), click in the text box (F) and type a name for the folder and click **OK** (G).

3. The new folder will then appear in the Folders List.

Rename a Folder

1. In the Folders List right-click the folder and from the drop-down list, click on **Rename** (J in Fig. 8).
2. Delete the old name and type in a new one for the folder. Click **OK**.

Deleting a Folder

You can only delete folders that you have created.
1. In the folders list, right-click the folder to be deleted and from the drop-down list click on **Delete** (I in Fig. 8).
2. Click on **Yes** to confirm deletion.

Moving Messages into Folders

1. Highlight the message in the message list (E in Fig. 9) and then click and drag it into a folder in the Folders List.
2. When the folder turns blue, release the button and the message will be dropped into its new position.

Deleting a Message and Emptying the Deleted Items Folder

1. In the message list click on the email to be removed (E in Fig. 9).
2. Click on the **Delete** button (D) and the email is sent to the **Deleted items** folder.
3. To restore a message from the Deleted items folder (A), click on the folder in the folders list, highlight the message in the message list and then click and drag the email back into its original folder.
4. To empty the Deleted items folder (A), right-click on the folder and then on **Empty 'Deleted items' folder** (F).

Sorting Messages

1. Use the message headers to sort your emails according to From, Subject and Date.
2. Click on the header button (e.g. C for From) and the list of emails will be rearranged in ascending or descending order.

Searching for a Message

1. Click in the **Search box** (B) and type in a word included in the message.
2. As you type, messages that correspond to your search will be listed.
3. If you still cannot find the relevant email click the **Search in:** button and select from the drop-down list.

Printing from Windows Live Mail

The printing from Windows Live Mail is very similar to a Word document – see Chapter Six.
1. In the message list, double-click on the message you wish to print.
2. Click on the **Print** button on the toolbar.
3. The Print dialog box opens.
4. Select a **Page Range** and the number of copies required.
5. Click on **Apply** and then on **Print**.

Section 7:
Attachments

You can attach documents, photographs and other files stored on your computer to an email in order to send them. But be aware that some ISPs will block over-large attachments. If you are going to attach a large file it's better to compress it first (see Chapter Four, Section 11).

Attach a Document

1. Click on the **Attach** button (A in Fig. 10) on the toolbar.
2. The Open box is displayed.
3. Locate and select your document.
4. Click on **Open**. The Open box closes and the file is attached (B).

Attach a Photo

When a photo is attached to an email, it is placed in the body of the email and can be viewed by the recipient by scrolling down the message.

1. Click on the **Add photos** button (C in Fig. 10) and navigate to the folder that contains your photos. Select the photo, click on **Add** and then **Done**.
2. Use the formatting tools on the photos toolbar to make alterations to your photos, e.g. add a frame (D), rotate, autocorrect (E).
3. To add a title, move the cursor over the photo and the **Click here to add text** box appears (F).
4. Click on the **Layout** button (G) to change the layout of pictures and text.
5. Click on the arrows (H) to expand the toolbar.

Opening, Saving and Printing an Attachment

1. Highlight the message (A in Fig. 11).

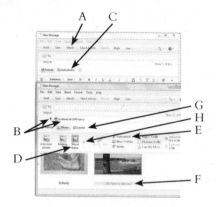

Fig. 10

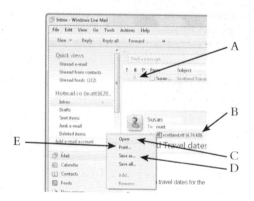

Fig. 11

2. Right-click on the name of the attachment (B).

3. Click on **Open** (C) to view the attachment.

4. Click on **Save as** (D) and the **Save Attachment As** box opens.

5. Navigate to the folder where you wish to save the attachment.

6. Click on the **Save** button.

7. To print the attachment click on **Print** (E).

Warning: be very wary of opening attachments from people you do not know or organisations you have never heard of. An email attachment is one of the most common methods of spreading a computer virus and spoof emails are increasingly used in attempted fraud. If you are suspicious, delete the email and do not open any attachments. Better to be safe than sorry.

Section 8:
Customising Receiving, Reading and Sending Email

Decide how Windows Live Mail deals with your messages

1. Click on **Tools** (C in Fig. 12) on the menu bar, then click on **Options** in the drop-down menu (A).

2. Click on the **Read** (E) and **Send** (G) tabs to select options for reading and sending emails. Click to place a tick in the check boxes (B) by those that you wish to keep.

3. Click on the **General** tab (D) to select options for receiving email.

4. When you have finished making your selections, click **Apply** and then **OK** (I).

C D E F G H

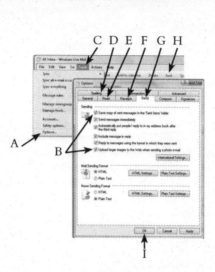

Fig. 12

Request a Receipt

If you wish to be notified when your emails reach their recipients, you can request a receipt.

1. Open the **Options** box as above. Click on the **Receipts** tab (F in Fig. 12).

2. Click the check box by **Request a read receipt for all sent messages**.

3. Click **Apply** and then **OK**.

Section 9:
Email Safety, Junk Emails and Phishing

Email is a great way to communicate but it's important to be vigilant against spam and junk emails, and those that carry attachments with viruses. Another concern is phishing, whereby spoof emails are sent to unsuspecting recipients, with deliberate intent to commit fraud – often using international domains. Windows Live Mail comes with various tools to help you stay safe. (See also Chapter Ten on Security.)

Junking Unwanted Emails

If you receive any that emails that Windows Live Mail identifies as suspect it will direct them into your Junk email folder. If you receive other unwanted emails, future messages from the same sender can be sent to the Junk email folder or filtered there automatically.

1. Click on the unwanted email.
2. Click on the **Junk** button (H in Fig. 12) of the toolbar.

To Block and Filter Unwanted Emails Automatically

1. Highlight the email and click on **Actions** on the menu bar.
2. Click on **Junk e-mail** and then on **Add sender to blocked senders list**.
3. Click **OK** and the email will be removed to the Junk email folder and the sender added to the **Blocked Senders List**.

4. Future emails from the sender will be filtered automatically into the Junk email folder from where they can be deleted, unopened.

Not Junk after all!

Sometimes Windows Live Mail will classify a safe email as junk. Check the Junk email folder frequently, just in case a genuine email has been filtered into it. If you decide that an email is not junk after all it's easy to return it to the Inbox.

1. Click on the **Junk E-mail** folder in the folders list.
2. Highlight the message concerned. Click on the **Not Junk** button on the toolbar and the message will be sent to the Inbox.

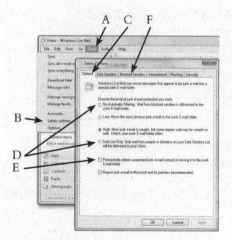

Fig. 13

Setting Safety Options

1. Click on **Tools** (A in Fig. 13) on the menu bar.

2. Click on **Safety options** (B).

3. On the **Options** tab (C), click on an option button to select a level of junk email protection (D).

4. It's best not to select the check box (E) by **Permanently delete suspected junk e-mail**. If you haven't checked the Junk email folder recently you may end up deleting safe emails that have been wrongly filtered. Once deleted they cannot be retrieved.

5. Click on **Apply** and then **OK**.

Adding or Removing from the Blocked Senders List

1. On the **Safety Options** box click on the **Blocked Senders** tab (F).

2. To remove an address, highlight it and click the **Remove** button.

3. Click on **Apply** and then **OK**.

4. To add an email address to Blocked Senders, click on **Add** and then type or copy and paste the address into the **Add address or domain** box. Click **OK**.

5. Click **Apply** and then **OK** on the Safety Options box.

Protection against Phishing and Virus Attacks

1. On the **Safety Options** box click on the **Phishing** tab.

2. Click to place a tick in the check box by **Protect my Inbox from messages with potential Phishing links** and by **Move Phishing e-mail to the Junk e-mail folder**.

3. Click on **Apply** and then **OK**.

4. To discover more click on the link **Click here to learn more about phishing**.

5. To block international junk email click on the **International** tab.

6. Click the **Blocked Top Level Domain List**.

7. Click the check boxes to place a tick against those domains to be blocked.

8. Click **OK** and then **Apply** and **OK** on the Safety Options box.

9. Click on the **Security** tab.

10. Select the level of security that you want by clicking on the option buttons or check boxes. Click **Apply** and then **OK**.

Section 10:
Managing your Contacts

Windows Live Contacts enables you to add email addresses from your contacts and other details that are useful to you.

Adding a New Email Address

1. Click on the **Contacts** button (A in Fig. 14) in the folders pane.

2. Click on the **New** button (B) on the toolbar.

3. On the **Add a Contact** box type in the name and email address (C) of your contact and any other details. Click on the **Add contact** button.

4. Click on the **Close** button to close **Windows Live Contacts**.

Edit a Contact

1. Click on the **Contacts** button (A in Fig. 14) in the folders pane.
2. Click on **Edit** (D). Click on a category on the left and enter details in the text boxes on the right of the box. Click **Save**.

Adding an Address from an Email

1. In the Message list right-click the email. On the drop-down menu click on **Add sender to contacts**.
2. In the reading pane you will also find the **Add contact** link under the name and email address of the sender.

Adding Email Addresses Automatically

1. Click on **Tools** on the menu bar, click **Options**.
2. Click on the **Send** tab. Add a tick to the check box by **Automatically put people I reply to in my address book after the third reply**. Click on **Apply** and then **OK**. To close this window click on the **Close** button (E in Fig. 14).

Section 11:
Windows Calendar

Windows Calendar is an integral part of Window Live Mail and helps you to organise and keep track of your activities. You can have more than one calendar, one of them being the primary calendar.

Open and View Windows Calendar

1. Open Windows Live Mail.
2. In the folder pane click on **Calendar** (A in Fig. 15).

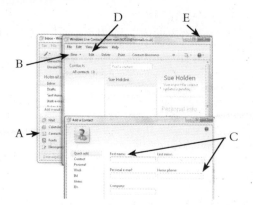

Fig. 14

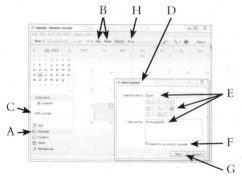

Fig. 15

3. The calendar opens showing Month view.

4. Click on **Day** or **Week** (B) buttons to change the view.

Add a Calendar

1. Click on **Add calendar** (C) in the navigation pane and the **Add a Calendar** box opens (D).

2. Enter a name for the calendar and a description (E).

3. Tick a colour for the calendar (E).

4. Clear or tick the check box by **Make this my primary calendar** (F).

5. Click **Save** (G).

Print a Calendar

1. Click on the **Print** button on the toolbar (H in Fig. 15).

2. Select **Print Style, Print Range** and **Number of copies** on the Print box.

3. Click **OK**.

Change a Calendar's Name or Delete

1. Move the mouse over the calendar name (A in Fig. 16) in the navigation pane and a drop-down arrow appears.

2. Click on the arrow and then on **Properties** (B).

3. Make your desired changes and then click **Save**.

4. To delete the calendar completely, click on **Delete** (C).

Make an Appointment or Add an Event

1. Click on the calendar concerned in the navigation pane.

2. Find the month for the appointment by clicking on the back/forward buttons.

Fig. 16

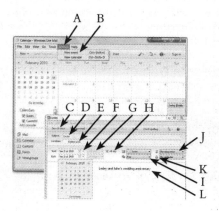

Fig. 17

3. Click on the required date for the appointment. Start typing and a text box appears containing your text.

4. To add an appointment that might last all day or that reoccurs at regular intervals, click on **Actions** (A in Fig. 17) on the menu bar and then click **New event** (B).

5. Type in a **Subject** (D) and a **Location** (E).

6. Click on the downward arrow by **Start** (F) and from the calendar click on a date. Repeat for the **End** date.

7. Click on the spin buttons (G) to select the start and finish times of the appointment.

8. For an all-day appointment click the **All day** check box (H).

9. Click the **Free/Busy** button (I). Other people who are allowed to view your calendar will then be able to see your availability for the event.

10. Click on the arrow by **No Recurrence** (J) and select how often this appointment is to be kept.

11. For an advance reminder, click the arrow by **No Reminder** (K) and select from the drop-down list.

12. Type in details of the appointment or event (L).

13. Click the **Save & Close** button (C).

Email an Appointment

1. Click on the calendar in the navigation pane.

2. Locate the date of the appointment and click on it.

3. Click on the **Send in e-mail** button on the toolbar.

4. The email window opens with details of the event.

5. Add the email address of the recipients and click on **Send**.

Deleting a Calendar Entry

1. To delete an appointment, click on the date of the entry and then click on the **Delete** button.

2. Another way to delete an entry is to right-click the appointment and click on **Delete** on the drop-down list.

Chapter Thirteen:
Maintaining Your Computer

Windows 7 has tools to help you keep your computer
system operating efficiently and effectively, to maintain
and check its performance and if necessary take any
recommended remedial action. If regular checks are
not done, you may find your computer starts to operate
more slowly and/or that some programs do not respond.
Maintenance tasks should be done on a regular basis. This
chapter covers four main areas:

Maintaining your Hard Drive: Checking,
cleaning and defragmenting your hard drive will keep it
working more sharply (see sections 1–3).

Creating Safeguards: Guard against any future
problems by learning how to use system restore and
ensuring that you use back-up to keep copies of your
personal files (see sections 4–6).

**Troubleshooting, Corrections, Restoring
Files, Repairs and Removing Errors:**
Familiarise yourself with the tools to help repair and correct
problems *before* a problem occurs (see sections 7–13).

**Conserve Energy and Maximise
Performance Using Power Plans:** Choose
a power plan to conserve energy while getting the best
performance out of your computer (see section 14).

Section 1:
Error-checking your Disk to Find and Fix Errors

Use Error-checking to scan your hard disk for problems and to automatically repair any damage. It's a good idea to perform this process periodically: the hard drive will inevitably accrue 'bad sectors' due to various incidents such as program errors. You will not be able to use your computer while error-checking takes place.

1. Go to the **Start** menu and click on **Computer**.

2. Click on **Hard Disk Drive** (A in Fig. 1) and then **Properties** (B) on the toolbar.

3. Click on the **Tools** tab (A in Fig. 2) of the **Properties** dialog box.

4. Click on the **Check now** button (B) in the error-checking section of the tab.

5. Click to place a tick in the check boxes: **Automatically fix file systems errors** and **Scan for and attempt recovery of bad sectors** (C). Click **Start** (D).

6. Error-checking cannot take place while the computer is being used. A box will display requesting that checking is done next time the computer starts up. Click on **Schedule disk check**.

7. When you next you start up the computer disk checking will automatically begin.

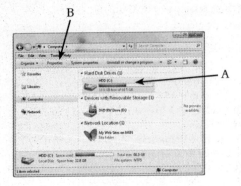

Fig. 1

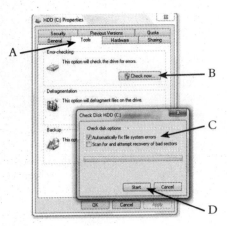

Fig. 2

Checking your Disk Space

Adding programs, pictures, files and documents to your computer inevitably reduces the amount of available space on your computer's hard drive. The same applies to removable disks and memory devices. It's quick and easy to check the amount of available space.

1. Click on the **Start** menu and click on **Computer**.

2. Click on the hard drive or disk (A in Fig. 3) that you are checking.

3. Click on **Properties** (B) on the toolbar.

4. On the **Properties** dialog box click on the **General** tab (C) (if not already open).

5. This clearly shows how much free and used space remains (D).

Note: if you are checking a removable device don't forget to insert it into the computer.

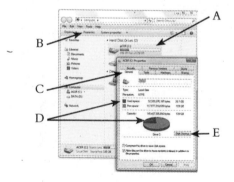

Fig. 3

Section 2:
Disk Cleanup – Getting Rid of Unwanted Files

You may decide to clean up your disk by deleting unwanted files and thus increase the amount of available space. Disk Cleanup identifies files that can safely be deleted, but make sure that you really do wish to remove them, as once they are gone they cannot be retrieved.

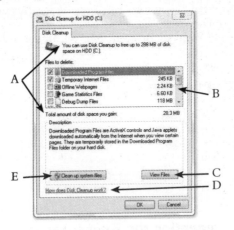

Fig. 4

1. Go to the **Start** menu and click on **Computer**.
2. Click on the **Hard Disk Drive** and click on **Properties** on the toolbar, then click on the **General** tab.

3. Click on **Disk cleanup** (E in Fig. 3). A progress bar will appear while disk cleanup calculates and displays how much space can be freed up (A in Fig. 4).
4. Select the files to be deleted (B).
5. Click on **View Files** (C) to see the contents of a folder
6. To clean up system files, click on the button **Clean up system files** (E).Wait while the progress bar makes its calculations.
7. Click **OK**.

*Note: for more information on Disk Cleanup click on **How does Disk Cleanup work?** (D). Disk Cleanup can also be accessed through **All Programs, Accessories,** and then **System Tools**.*

Section 3: Defragmenting

When a file is saved onto your hard drive the computer will use the first available space it finds and then save the rest elsewhere. Consequently, a file could be divided into many fragments. Eventually this fragmenting of files slows down the computer. Defragmenting (defragging for short) collects the pieces of individual files together, thus speeding up the computer.

Defragmenting the Hard Drive
1. Click on the **Start** menu, **Computer**, **Hard Disk Drive**, and then on **Properties** on the toolbar. Click on the **Tools** tab of the **Properties** dialog box.
2. Click on **Defragment Now** and the **Disk Defragmenter** window opens.

3. Click on **Analyze disk** (C in Fig. 5) to determine if your disk needs defragging.

4. The disk defragmenter is run on a schedule by default. If a schedule has not already been set, click on **Configure schedule** (A).

5. Use the drop-down lists to set the frequency, day and time for the schedule to automatically defragment (E). Click **OK** (F).

6. To override scheduled defragging, click on **Defragment disk** (D).

7. To stop the defragmenting process, click **Stop operation**.

8. The progress of defragging will be listed in the **Current status:** section of the window (B).

9. Windows will inform you when the process has finished.

Note: defragmenting can take a while. Pick a time when the computer is not in use.

Section 4:
Restore Points

System restore is a program you can use to correct your computer should problems occur. Sometimes installing new software or programs can upset the hard drive. Windows 7 creates restore points automatically at various times but its always a good idea to create your own restore point before installing new programs, adding new hardware or downloading programs or other files from the Internet. If your computer subsequently starts to operate in an inconsistent or unusual way, you can restore your

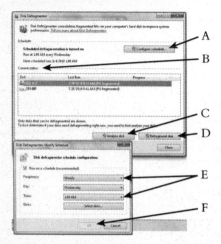

Fig. 5

computer to a date prior to installation or download, when it was working correctly.

Setting your own Restore Point

1. Click on **Start** and then **Computer** and the Computer window opens.

2. Click on **System Properties** on the toolbar and the System window opens. Click on **System protection** (A in Fig. 6) to open the **System Properties** dialog box.

3. Under the section **Protection Settings**, click on the **Create** button (B).

4. Type in a description (C). The date and time are added automatically.

5. Click **Create** (D). A progress bar will be displayed as the restore date is created.

6. A box will inform you that the restore point was successfully created. Click on **Close**.

Fig. 6

Section 5:
Creating Back-up Files

Should your computer become badly corrupted, infected by a virus or suffer any type of disastrous damage, having back-up copies will mean not losing vital work or important personal files. Windows 7 has made it easier than ever to keep back-up files. If you wish to just back-up a small number of selected files you can use a CD or DVD;

a USB memory device will hold more information and would be useful to back-up picture files. However, to back-up all your data Microsoft recommends an external hard drive, many of which are now available at very reasonable prices and come with plug and play – so they are easy to use. When back-up has been completed the device can be removed and stored in a safe place.

Setting up Backup

1. Click on **Start**. Type **Backup** in the Search box of the Start menu.

2. Click on **Backup and Restore**.

3. Click on **Set up backup** (A in Fig. 7).

4. A progress bar will appear and then **Set up backup** will open.

5. You will need to decide where you are going to save your back-up files. Click on the link **Guidelines for choosing a backup destination** (B) for more information about devices to use.

6. Make sure the device you have chosen is attached to the computer.

7. Click an option button to decide whether to let Windows choose which files and data to back-up or to select the files yourself.

8. If you select **Let Windows choose**, click on **Next**. (If you are choosing which files to select for back-up click on **Next** and then select the files by clicking on the check boxes next to them. Click **Next**.)

9. **Review your backup settings** (A in Fig. 8) – if you wish to change anything click on the **Back** button (B). If you wish to change the time and frequency of automatic backup, click on **Change schedule** (C).

10. Click on **Save settings and run backup** (D) to run for the first time.

Section 6:
Using Backup after Set-up

Once you have set up Backup you may wish to add a different device as extra or further back-up or one of the devices that you already use may become full. Back up is easy to manage or to change.

1. Insert backup CD/ USB device or plug in any external disk that is being used.
2. Open **Backup and Restore** and click **Backup now** (E in Fig. 8), which will scan for new or updated files and add them to your back-up disk.
3. If your current back-up disk or device becomes full, insert a new device, open **Backup and Restore,** click on **Change settings** (F) and select the new location for your back-up. Click **Next** and continue the back-up process.

Suspending Automatic Backup
1. Open up Backup and Restore.
2. Click on **Turn off schedule** (G).

Section 7:
Check your Security Settings

Some computer problems may indicate an infection; for example, programs may not respond normally or the computer may suddenly shut down. Before you attempt any repair, check that there's no infection by scanning your computer using your anti-virus program and Windows Defender; ensure that all your security features are turned on as covered in Chapter Ten.

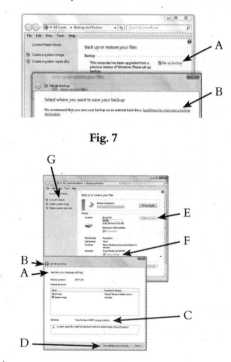

Fig. 7

Fig. 8

Section 8:
Find and Use a Troubleshooter

Windows 7 has a whole raft of troubleshooters and they all follow a similar format. We disconnected from the Internet to create a specific problem as an illustration.

1. Click on **Start**, click on **Control Panel** and then in category view (A in Fig. 9) under **System and Security**, click on **Find and fix problems** (B).

2. We clicked on **Network and Internet** (C) to view a list of trouble shooters and then clicked on **Internet Connections** (A in Fig. 10).

3. We clicked on **Next** (B) on the Troubleshooter.

4. A progress bar appeared while the problem was being detected.

5. The Troubleshooter then asked us to **Select the issue windows should troubleshoot**.

6. Whichever Troubleshooter you are using, at this stage, you need to choose a solution and then click on it.

7. If the Troubleshooter offers a solution, click **Apply this Fix** or **Skip this step continue trying to fix the problem**, if the solution is not what you need.

8. The Troubleshooter will continue to look for solutions; follow the instructions as they appear, making any changes suggested and which you think you need.

Fig. 9

Fig. 10

Section 9:
Correcting your System with System Restore

This program allows you to undo any changes made to your computer, returning it to a date when it was working normally. You will not lose any of your personal files (as long as you have saved them), but you may lose any recently downloaded or installed software.

1. Type System Restore in the Start menu Search box.
2. The **System Restore** wizard opens. Click on **Next**.
3. Click the check box (A in Fig. 11) to view more restore points (B).
4. Click on a date predating the current problem. Click on **Next** (C).
5. On the System Restore window, click to select the disk that needs restoring – usually the computer's hard disk. Click on **Finish**.
6. A warning box is displayed stating **Once started System Restore cannot be interrupted**. Click on **Yes** to continue.
7. A progress bar is displayed; the computer shuts down and then automatically reopens and is restored to the date that you have chosen.
8. Log in and then click **OK** on the confirmation box.

Note: if System Restore was not successful it will recommend you choose a different restore point.

Fig. 11

Section 10:
Windows Memory Diagnostic Tool

Any defect in the computer's memory may result in
losing information; the computer may even stop working.
Windows 7 works to keep the computer's memory intact by
continually checking for any possible memory problems. If
it detects something wrong, you will receive a notification.
1. Click on the notification.
2. Click on **Restart now and check for problems
(recommended)** (A in Fig. 12).
3. Save any work and close any open programs. (If you do
not wish to be interrupted at this point select **Check for
problems the next time I start my computer**.)
4. The computer will shut down and then restart.
5. **Windows Memory Diagnostic Tool** will appear on the
screen showing a progress bar and the status of the memory.

6. When completed the computer will shut down again and then restart automatically.

7. Log on and a notification will appear with the results of the test (B).

Extra: you can check your computer's memory at any time. Click in the Start Search box and type in diagnostic, and the tool will be listed on the Start menu. Click on it to open.

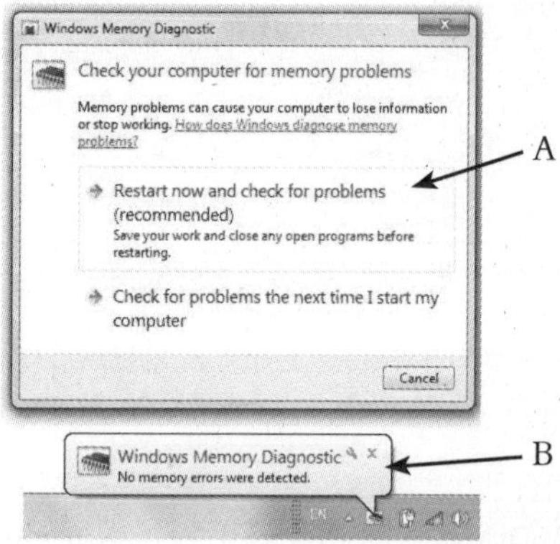

Fig. 12

Section 11:
Repair, Uninstall or Change a Program

Sometimes software programs on your computer can become corrupted or damaged, or you may wish to uninstall a program that you are no longer using. First, you need to view the programs that are installed on your system.

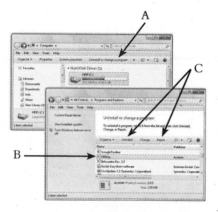

Fig. 13

Viewing the Programs on your Computer

1. Click on **Start**, click on **Computer**.

2. Click on **Uninstall or change a program** (A in Fig. 13).

3. Scroll down the list of programs until you find one that you need to repair, change or uninstall (B).

4. Click to highlight the program. The row of buttons on the command bar at the top of the list of programs will be different for each individual program but they will include **Organize, Uninstall, Change** and **Repair** (C).

5. A program cannot always be repaired but if it can, then the **Repair** button appears.

6. Click on the appropriate button for any other action such as **Uninstall** or **Change**.

7. Whichever you choose, follow the instructions as they appear on the screen.

Note: you may be requested to reinstall the program CD or go online to repair any damage.

Restoring Files

If you have accidentally deleted or lost your files or folders then it is very simple to restore them using the Backup and Restore wizard. (This only works, of course, if you have been regularly backing-up your files.)

Section 12:
Restoring Backed-up Folders

1. Attach the device you used for your back-up.

2. Click on **Start**. Type **Backup** in the Search box of the Start menu.

3. Click on **Backup and Restore** on the menu and the **Backup and Restore** window opens.

4. Click on **Browse for folders** (B in Fig. 14).

5. In the navigation pane click the back-up to be used (A in Fig. 15).

6. If you don't wish to restore the whole back-up double-click the folders (B) in the contents pane until you locate the one you wish to restore.

7. Single-click the folder, then click on **Add folder** (C).

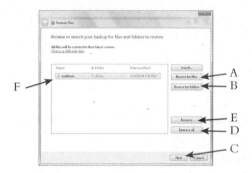

Fig. 14

Fig. 15

8. If you wish to remove a folder/s from the restore list, highlight (F in Fig. 14) and then click on **Remove** (E) or **Remove all** (D). Click **Next** (C).

9. Click on the radio button to restore the file **In the original location**.

10. If you are asked if you want to copy and replace files Click on **Copy and Replace** if you want to update your files or **Copy, but keep both files**.

11. A progress bar appears and then a window opens informing you that your files and folders have been successfully restored.

12. Click **Restore** and then **Finish**.

Restoring Backed-up Files

1. Follow steps 1–3 above.

2. Click on **Browse for files** (A in Fig. 14), then click **Next** (C).

3. In the navigation pane, click the back-up to be used.

4. In the contents pane, select a folder. Double-click or click **Open folder** to open until you locate the file you wish to restore.

5. Click on the file and then on the **Add files** button.

6. Click on **Next**.

7. Follow the steps 8–12 above.

Section 13:
Use Restart to Solve a Problem

Minor problems can sometimes be solved by using Restart. First, if possible, save any work and close the program you are using.

1. Click on **Start**, click on the arrow next to the power button.

2. Click on **Restart**.

3. Windows 7 will close down and restart automatically.

Section 14:
Conserve Energy and Maximise Performance Using Power Plans

By choosing a power plan you can conserve the battery on your laptop or the electrical consumption of a desktop. There are three power plans to choose from: **Balanced**, **Power saver** and **High performance**, or you can create your own power plan. **Balanced** is the recommended default plan. Be aware that if you wish to change to another plan the computer may lose a little in performance.

Opening the Power Options Window
Click on the **Start** button, then on **Control Panel** and in large or small icons view click on **Power Options**.

Select a Power Plan
1. Your computer will probably show that **Balanced (recommended)** (A in Fig. 16) has already been selected.
2. Click on the arrow by **Hide additional plans** (C) to see or hide further plans.
3. Use the slider control to adjust the screen brightness (D).
4. Select a plan by clicking on the option button (E) next to it and then choose the settings by clicking on **Change plan settings** (B).
5. On the new window that opens click on the down arrows (A in Fig. 17) and choose the length of time that elapses to: **Dim the display, Turn off the display**, and **Put the computer to sleep**. (You can save power by putting the computer to sleep after a specified period of non-use.)

6. Use the slider control to **Adjust plan brightness** (B).

7. Click on **Save changes** (C).

*Note: to return a plan to the original settings click on **Restore default settings for this plan**.*

Sending the Computer to Sleep and Turning off the Display

This can be done without changing previous power plans or creating a new one. Just open the **Power Options** window as above and click on **Choose when to turn off the display** or **Change when the computer sleeps** (F in Fig. 16).

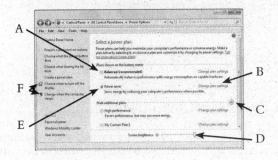

Fig. 16

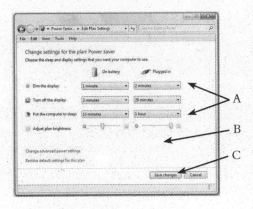

Fig. 17

Chapter Fourteen:
Using External Hardware

When you add a new piece of hardware to your set-up it needs to be detected by the computer. Windows 7 is designed to detect most new devices and pieces of hardware automatically. The latest range are known as 'plug and play' and most plug into a USB port; some come with installation discs. However, if you try to attach an older piece of equipment you may need to use the **Add a Device** wizard.

Section 1:
Adding a New Device

Add a Plug and Play Device
1. Just plug the device into the computer terminal (following any instructions accompanying the device).
2. Windows 7 automatically finds and installs it and it is ready to use.

Adding New Hardware that Comes with an Installation CD
1. Read the instructions that came with the CD.
2. Plug the device into the correct port as recommended by the manufacturer (probably a USB port), insert the CD and follow any prompts.
3. If a User Account Control permissions box appears, click **Continue**. You may need to follow the manufacturer's

instructions as they appear on screen. This will probably include accepting a licence agreement.

4. A progress bar will indicate the status of the installation process.

5. You may be requested to restart your computer to complete installation.

6. Once the computer has restarted, you will need to log on.

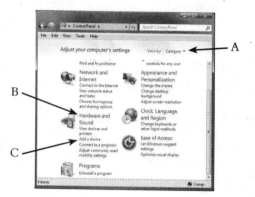

Fig. 1

Using the Add a Device Wizard

If Windows 7 did not automatically detect the new device you can use the **Add a device** wizard. This searches through all the computer's systems to find and make the device operational.

1. Make sure you have plugged the device into the computer.
2. Go to **Start**, and click on **Control Panel** and in category view (A in Fig. 1) under **Hardware and Sound** (B), click on **Add a device** (C).
3. Windows will search for any new devices and then display them.
4. Click on the device you wish to install. Click on **Next**.
5. Follow the instructions as they appear on the screen – these vary with each device.

View Devices and Printers

1. To see what devices are already installed on your computer, click on **Start, Control Panel** and in category view under **Hardware and Sound**, click on **View devices and printers**.
2. Click on a device and its details appear in the Details pane (A in Fig. 2).
3. On the command bar are the buttons **Add a device** and **Add a printer** (B). Other buttons may also be displayed and vary according to the type of device you have selected.
4. Right-click a device (C) and the drop-down menu enables you to **Create shortcut** (D) to the device on the desktop, to **Troubleshoot** (E) and view its **Properties** (F).
5. Click on **Properties** (F). There are a number of tabs, which vary with different devices.
The **Hardware** tab (A in Fig. 3) gives the device status and states whether it is working properly (B).

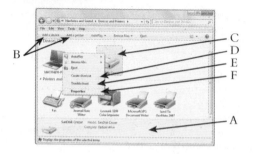

Fig. 2

Fig. 3

Section 2:
Troubleshooting and Device
Software Updates

Troubleshooting Hardware

1. Click on **Start,** click on **Control Panel** and in category view, under **Hardware and Sound**, click on **View devices and printers**.

2. If there is a yellow warning icon displayed next to a piece of hardware, check that the cables and connections are in place.

3. If the yellow warning remains, click on the troubleshoot button on the toolbar or right-click the device and click on **Troubleshoot** on the drop-down menu and follow the instructions as they appear.

Extra: if the problem remains it may help to uninstall the device through the computer and then reinstall it again – do not just disconnect the device. Also try the manufacturer's website, which should have help, troubleshooting or FAQ pages, and maybe a phone number of a helpline (check first for cost).

Staying Up to Date with Device Software

Manufacturers are continually improving the software that comes with devices, so it's a good idea to periodically update those you have installed on your computer in order to get maximum benefit. To do this you need to open the **Device Manager**. Make sure you are connected to the Internet as this process will lead you to the manufacturer's website.

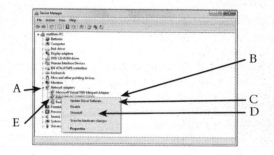

Fig. 4

1. In the Start menu Search box, type in **Device** and the **Device Manager** is displayed in the Start menu. Click on it to open.

2. Click on an arrow (A in Fig. 4) to expand a folder, and locate your device.

3. Right-click on the name of your device (e.g. E in Fig. 4). A drop-down menu (B) appears.

4. Click on **Update Driver Software** (C).

5. Click on **Search automatically for updated driver software**. If your software is up to date Windows will inform you. If not, it will search online and download the necessary software.

6. You will probably need to restart your computer to complete installation.

Section 3:
Uninstalling or Removing a Device

Uninstalling Hardware Drivers

When you uninstall a device you also need to uninstall the driver that operates the device.

1. Open the Device Manager as in Section 2 above.

2. Right-click on the name of your device. A drop-down menu (B in Fig. 4) displays.

3. Click on **Uninstall** (D).

4. A Warning box is displayed. Make sure that you are uninstalling the correct driver for the software of the device – if you are not sure, click **Cancel**. Otherwise click **OK**.

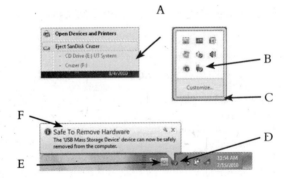

Fig. 5

Ejecting and Removing Plug and Play Devices

1. On the notification area of the taskbar is the **Safely Remove Hardware and Eject Media** icon (D in Fig. 5).
2. If you cannot see it, click on the **Show hidden icons** arrow (E) to view the hidden icons list (C).
3. Locate the **Safely Remove Hardware and Eject Media** icon (B) and click on it.
4. Click on **Eject** (A) by the name of the device on the pop-up list.
5. The computer disengages the device and notifies you (F) that it's safe to remove the device.
6. Unplug the device.

Section 4: Adding a Printer to your Set-up

If you have a Plug and Play or USB printer, Windows 7 will automatically find and set up your printer without you needing to do anything.

1. Plug the printer's cable into the computer terminal.
2. Ensure the printer is plugged into the mains and is switched on.
3. Check to see if your printer has an 'On' button. Ensure it is switched on.
4. Windows 7 will detect your new hardware and install it.
5. If your printer was not detected, and some are not, then use one of the **Add a Printer Wizards** as described below.

Add a Local Printer Wizard

Use this wizard if your printer does not have a USB connection and you are attaching it to just one computer.

1. Go to **Start**, and click on **Control Panel**. Select **Category** next to **View by:** (A in Fig 1).

2. Click on **Hardware and Sound,** and then click on the category **Devices and Printers** and a new window opens.

3. On the toolbar click on **Add a printer** (A in Fig. 6).

4. Select **Add a local printer** (B). Use this option only if your printer does not have a USB connection.

5. **Choose a printer port** is displayed. A recommended port will already be listed.

6. Click on **Next**.

7. **Install the printer driver** is displayed. Select the manufacturer (A in Fig. 7) and the name of your printer (B). Scroll to see more names.

8. Either click **Next** and follow step 9 below or if you have an installation disk click **Have Disk** (C). The **Install from Disk box** opens. Insert the disk and follow the instructions as they appear on the screen.

9. The name should be automatically listed in the **Printer name** box; if not, type in the name. Click **Next** and a progress bar appears as the printer is installed.

10. Click an option button by either **Do not share this printer** or **Share this printer so that others on your network can find and use it**.

11. The wizard will tell you that you have successfully added a printer. Make sure the check box is ticked by **Set as the default printer**.

12. Click on **Print a test page**. Click on **Finish**.

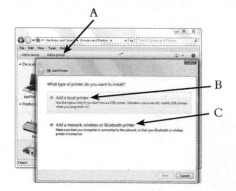

Fig. 6

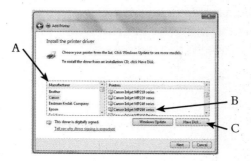

Fig. 7

Add a Network, Wireless or Bluetooth Printer Wizard

If your printer is part of a network, make sure that your computer is connected to the network. If it is a wireless or Bluetooth printer, make sure it is switched on.

1. Follow actions 1–3 above for **Add a Local Printer Wizard**.
2. Click **Add a network, wireless or Bluetooth printer** (C in Fig. 6). Follow the instructions as they are displayed on the screen.
3. If the wizard hasn't found the printer, click on **The printer that I want isn't listed**.
4. Click on **Browse** and browse the network to find the printer to which you want to connect.
5. Follow the instructions as they are displayed on the screen.

Section 5:
Managing your Printer and Controlling the Printing

There may be times when you wish to cancel a printing job or perhaps check on the level of ink in the printer's cartridges. The printers window allows you to control the printing, adjust print options and also customise the printer to suit your requirements.

Opening the Printers Window

1. Go to **Start**, and click on **Control Panel**. Select **Category** next to **View by:** (A in Fig. 1).

2. Click on **Hardware and Sound**, and then click on the category **Devices and Printers**.

3. Double-click on the printer (A in Fig. 8) and its own window opens.

4. Not all printers will show the same options – it will depend on the manufacturer.

5. The window in Fig. 8 shows **See what's printing** (B), **Customize your printer** (F) and **Adjust print options** (G).

6. Some printers may show links called **Display Printer Properties** and **Display Print Queue**.

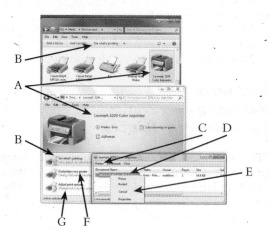

Fig. 8

The Printing Queue

It's easy to check on the documents in the printing queue and cancel or pause a printing job. The latter is useful if, for example, the printer has run out of paper or there is a paper jam.

1. Double-click on **See what's printing** (B in Fig. 8) or if applicable, **Display Print Queue**.

2. Right-click on a document (D) and select from the drop-down menu (E) **Cancel,** if you wish to cancel the print, **Pause**, or **Restart** (to restart printing).

3. If you wish to cancel all printing, click on **Printer** (C) on the menu bar, and then on the drop-down menu click on **Cancel All Documents**.

4. This may not stop all printing as a number of pages will have been sent to the printer and remain in its memory.

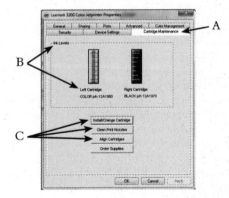

Fig. 9

Cartridge Maintenance

At some point you will need to replace or change the print cartridges. It's also a good idea to routinely clean the print nozzles as over time they can become clogged with ink and the print on a document can lose definition.

1. Click on **Customize your printer** (F in Fig. 8) or if applicable, **Display Printer Properties**.
2. The printing property box opens.
3. Click on the **Cartridge Maintenance** tab (A in Fig. 9) or if applicable, **Maintenance,** then click on the relevant buttons and follow the instructions.
4. In Fig. 9 the levels of ink can be seen at a glance (B). Click a button to **Install/ Change cartridge**, **Clean Print Nozzles** or **Align Cartridges** (C).
5. Follow the instructions as they appear on screen.

Adjust Print Options and Display Printer Properties

If your printer window shows **Adjust print options** follow steps 1–4 below. If it has the **Display Printer Properties** link, click on it and go to step 5.
1. Double-click on **Adjust print options** (G on Fig. 8). The printing preferences dialog box opens. The tabs available will depend on the printer installed.
2. The **Layout** tab (A in Fig. 10) enables paper orientation, page order and format to be selected.
3. The **Paper/Quality** (B) tab allows selection of ink colour, settings and paper source.
4. When you have made your selections click **Apply** and then **OK** (C).

5. Click on the **General tab**, the **Preferences** button and the **Page setup** tab.

6. Choose page size, orientation, layout and the number of copies to be printed. Click on **Apply** and **OK**.

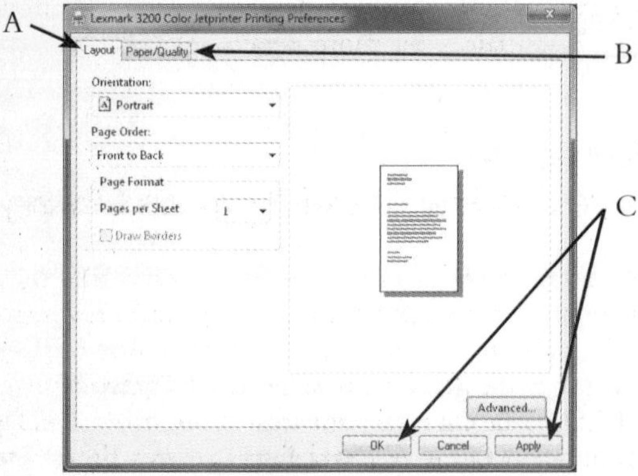

Fig. 10

Chapter Fifteen:
Pictures

Windows 7 comes pre-installed with the Pictures library and Windows Photo Viewer, enabling you to view and organise pictures downloaded from a digital camera or scanned in from a scanner. It's worth remembering that the Paint program can also be used to edit pictures. An improved and expanded Windows Live Photo Gallery is now available as a free download from Windows Live Essentials – for more details see Chapter Two, Section 13.

Section 1:
An Overview of the Pictures Library

The Pictures library can be used to create a slide show, view your pictures, add details, tags and star ratings, and to burn picture files to a disc.

1. Click on the **Start** menu and then on **Pictures**.

2. Click on the **Change your view** down arrow (F in Fig. 1) and select **Large** or **Extra Large** icons – these views make visually identifying pictures much easier.

3. In the folders list, click on **Pictures** (A), **Public Pictures** and then **Sample Pictures** folder (I). The pictures open in the contents pane.

4. Click on **Organize** (B) on the command bar and then on **Layout,** and on **Details pane** and **Preview pane**.

5. The **Details pane** (H) enables you to view further details about the picture file. To add more click on a field

and type your information in the text box that appears. (See Chapter Four, Fig. 15.)

6. The Preview pane (G) gives you a preview of any picture file that you click on without needing to open the whole file.

7. To copy a picture or folder to a disc, click on **Burn** (E) on the command bar.

Note: for more on burning to disc see Chapter Four, Section 14.

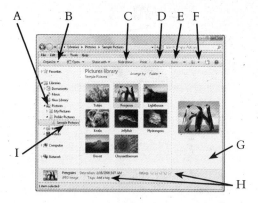

Fig. 1

Create a Slide Show

1. Click on a picture folder in the contents pane or the navigation pane or highlight a group of pictures in the contents pane.

2. Click on **Slide show** (C in Fig. 1).

3. The slide show is viewed in full screen.

4. If you don't want to wait for the next picture, left-click on the screen to progress through the show.

5. Right-click on the screen and use the list to navigate, **Pause** and **Play** (A in Fig. 2).

6. Use **Shuffle, Loop** and the **Speed** options (B) to customise your show.

7. Click on **Exit** (C) on the list to close the slide show.

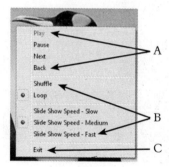

Fig. 2

Section 2:
Using Windows Photo Viewer and Emailing a Photo

Some email servers impose an upper limit of 1–2 megabytes per message so it's a good idea to resize your pictures before sending. Resizing does not affect the size of the original stored on your computer. If you need to send an image at high resolution, you may prefer to choose a larger size.

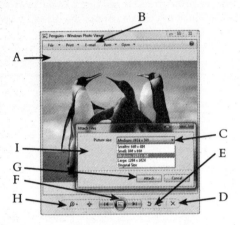

Fig. 3

1. Open the **Picture** library and then the **Sample Pictures** folder.

2. In the contents pane double-click on one of the pictures and it opens in **Windows Photo Viewer** (A in Fig. 3).

3. This allows you to move through a folder of pictures at your own pace and to zoom in on (H), rotate (E) and delete (D) a picture.

4. To email a picture click on **E-mail** (B) on the menu bar.

5. The **Attach Files** box (I) opens. Click on the down arrow (C) and select a size from the list.

6. Click on **Attach** (G) and Windows Live Mail or your default email program opens. (See Chapter Twelve, Section 1 on how to make an email program your default program.)
7. Add a recipient and click on **Send**.

*Note: to send more than one photo per message, open the Pictures folder, click and drag to highlight the group of pictures you wish to send and click on **E-mail** (D in Fig. 1) on the toolbar.*

Extra: if you click the play button (F in Fig. 3) on Windows Photo Viewer it begins a slide show.

Section 3:
Other Picture Programs on
Windows 7

Windows 7 also comes with Microsoft Office Picture Manager and Paint and these can be used for editing, making changes to your pictures or images and compressing a picture. For more on Paint see Chapter Nine, Section 3. To learn more about the Office Picture Manager, open the program, connect to the Internet and click on the **Help** button on the menu bar.

Open Other Picture Programs
1. Click on **Open** (A in Fig. 4) on the Picture library or on Windows Photo Viewer.
2. Click on the program (B) you wish to open and use.
3. If you used a CD to install software that came with your digital camera, that program will also be listed.

4. See Chapter Nine for Paint and Chapter Sixteen for Windows Media Center.

5. Use the Help and Support center to learn more about these other programs.

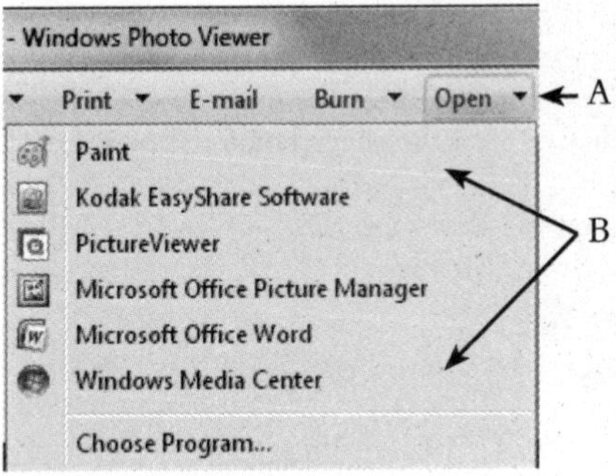

Fig. 4

Section 4:
Print a Photo

You can upload your photos from your camera onto the computer and then save them to a CD or a memory stick and take them to a photo developing shop to be processed. You can also print a photo using your own colour printer. To get a really good reproduction you need to use high quality glossy photographic paper, but you can still get an acceptable result from using good standard paper.

Pictures

1. Open your picture in the Picture library or Windows Photo Viewer.
2. Click on the **Print** button.
3. **Print Pictures** opens.
4. Click on the downward-pointing arrows (A in Fig. 5) to select the name of your **Printer**, **Paper size**, **Quality** and **Paper type**.
5. Use the spin buttons (B) to get the number of copies.
6. Click or clear the check box for **Fit picture to frame** (C).
7. Select the photo size (D).
8. Click on **Print** (E).

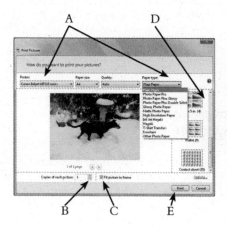

Fig. 5

Printing Multiple Photos

1. If you wish to print a number of different images, use the Picture library and click on the folder containing your photos in the navigation pane.

2. In the contents pane, click and drag to highlight the group of pictures to be printed.

3. If you wish to print all the images in a folder, click on **Organize** and then **Select all**.

Section 5:
Installing a Digital Camera or Scanner

Most digital cameras and scanners come with 'plug and play' – all you need to do is plug the device into a USB port in the computer and Windows 7 will automatically detect and install it. If your camera or scanner comes with an installation CD, then insert it and if the AutoPlay box appears, click on **Run Setup** and then follow the prompts as they appear on the screen. If your camera or scanner fails to install then you can use the Add a Device wizard.

1. Make sure you have plugged in your device and it is switched on.

2. Click on **Start,** click on **Devices and Printers** (alternatively click on **Control Panel** and in category view click on **Hardware and Sound** and then on the category **Devices and Printers**).

3. Click on the **Add a device** button on the toolbar.

4. The Add a device wizard searches for new devices.

5. Click the name of the camera or scanner and then click **Next**.

6. Follow the prompts as they appear on the screen.

Section 6:
Downloading from a Digital Camera

Once your camera has been plugged into the computer the downloading of the photographs should be automatic. They may be downloaded in **Camera Window** or in **AutoPlay**. You can also download in **Windows Live Photo Gallery** if this has been previously installed.

The Camera Window

1. Plug in the lead from your camera into the computer.
2. The Camera Window may display first as an icon (A in Fig. 6) on the taskbar.
3. Click on the icon to open.
4. Click on **Import pictures and videos** (B).
5. Give pictures a tag (C) if you wish.
6. Click on **Import** (D).

Fig. 6

AutoPlay

1. Plug in the lead from your camera to the computer.
2. The **AutoPlay** box opens.
3. Click on **Import Pictures**.
4. Give pictures a tag if you wish.
5. Click on **Import**.

Viewing your Downloaded Photos

1. Once the camera has finished downloading the **Pictures library** (B in Fig. 7) will open.
2. The photos will be contained in a folder labelled with the download date (A).
3. Click the folder and the pictures will open in the contents pane (C).

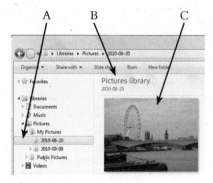

Fig. 7

Section 7:
Getting to Know Windows Live Photo Gallery

Windows Live Photo Gallery can be used to import pictures from your camera or scanner, organise your images, add captions and to do basic editing. It's not included as part of Windows 7 but can be downloaded for free – see Chapter Two, Section 13 for more details.

To Open Windows Live Photo Gallery
1. Click on **Start,** then onto **Windows Live Photo Gallery**.
2. If it isn't listed on the Start menu, type **photo** in the Search box and then click on the shortcut when it appears.

Organise and View your Pictures
The navigation pane allows you to sort your photos according to folders, date taken and tags.

Viewing
1. Open **Windows Photo Gallery**.
2. Click on **All photos and videos** (A in Fig. 8) to list the picture folders. Click on a folder to view the contents.
3. Click on **Date taken** (I) to view photos taken by year or by a month.
4. Click on tags (H) to view photos sorted in tag categories.
5. To view by ratings, click on the number of stars next to **Filter by** (D). Photos will be shown according to the rating you have selected.

6. To clear the rating filter, click on **Clear filter,** which replaces **Filter by**.

7. To search for a photo, type its name in the Search box (E) and pictures matching the text are displayed in the contents pane.

8. Use the controls (F) at the bottom of the window to zoom, rotate, delete and view details of a picture. Click and drag the slider to increase the size of a photo.

9. Click on **Info** (C) on the menu bar to see the information pane.

10. Click on **Fix** (B) on the menu bar to access the editing tools.

11. To see your pictures as a slide show, click on the slide show icon (G).

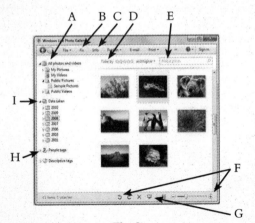

Fig. 8

Make a Copy of your Original Picture

1. In Windows Live Photo Gallery right-click on the image concerned and on the drop-down menu click on **copy**.
2. In the folders list, find the folder where you wish to save the copy, then right-click on it and on the drop-down menu click on **Paste**.

Section 8:
Creating a Slide Show Using Windows Live Photo Gallery

Use all the pictures in your collection or ones in selected folders to create a slide show.

1. Open Windows Live Photo Gallery and click on a folder.
2. Click on **Slide show** on the menu bar or on the slide show icon on the controls at the bottom of the window.
3. The screen is filled with a picture, gradually changing to the next picture contained within the folder.
4. Move the cursor to the bottom of the screen to use the slide show controls.
5. Use the controls to change the speed and theme of your slide show.

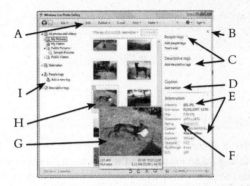

Fig. 9

Section 9:
Give a Picture a Star Rating, Add a Tag and Add a Caption

Tags, captions and star ratings help to categorise images and make it easier to organise and keep track of them. With Windows 7 this is now very easy to do.

1. Click on the **Info** button (A in Fig. 9) on the menu bar.

2. Click on the picture (H) that you wish to rate or add tags and a caption.

3. Click on **Add descriptive tags** or **Add people tags** (C) and in the text boxes that opens type your text.

4. Click on **Add caption** (D) and in the text box that opens type in a relevant caption.

5. To rate a picture, click on the number of stars (F) you want to give the image.

6. Click on any other field to add further information on author, date and file name (E).

7. Click on a picture and then allow the pointer to rest on the image. A larger version (G) is displayed giving details of the time and date the photo was taken.

8. Click on the **Close** (B) button to exit the Info pane.

Add a New Tag

1. Click **Add a new tag** (I in Fig. 9) in the navigation pane. Type the name of the tag. Press **Enter** on the keyboard.

2. Click a photo or select a group of photos and drag them into the tag.

3. Repeat the process with **Descriptive tags**.

4. When you click on a tag in the navigation pane only those photos within the tag will be displayed in the contents pane.

More on People Tags

People tags are really useful to help identify people in large group photographs.

1. Double-click on a photo.

2. Click on **Tag someone** (C in Fig. 10).

3. Move your cursor onto the photo and click.

4. A box (B) appears which can be moved onto the face of a person.

5. Click in the text box under **Tag someone** (A) and type a name and then press **Enter** on the keyboard to save.

6. When you next move the cursor over the photo a tag will appear identifying the people that you have tagged.

A   B   C

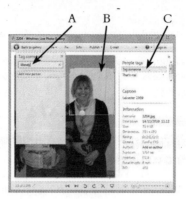

Fig. 10

Section 10:
Printing From Windows Live Photo Gallery

1. Open Windows Live Photo Gallery
2. Click on the picture you wish to print.
3. Click on the **Print** button on the menu bar and then on the drop-down menu click **Print**. The **Print Pictures** box opens.
4. Now follow the steps for printing from Pictures in Section 4 of this chapter.

Ordering Prints Online

1. Connect to the Internet and open Windows Live Photo Gallery.

2. Select your photos.

3. Click on **Print** on the menu bar and then on **Order prints**.

4. A list of online printing companies will be downloaded.

5. Make your selection, and follow the on screen prompts as they appear.

Section 11:
Downloading Photos in Windows Live Photo Gallery

1. Open **Windows Live Photo Gallery** and plug in your camera.

2. Click on **File** (A in Fig. 11) on the menu bar and click **Import from a camera or scanner** (B).

3. On the **Import Pictures and Videos** box click on the icon of the camera that you have plugged in.

4. Click on the **Import** button.

5. Select an option:

Import all new items now (D) will import all new photos on your camera.

- Click on the text box (E) to enter a name.
- Click on **Add tags** (G) if you wish to add a tag.
- Click on the **Import** button.

If you choose **Review, organize and group items to import** (C in Fig. 11), click on **Next** (F) and you can then select different groups of photos.

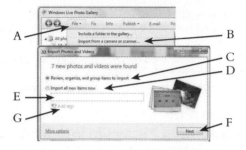

Fig. 11

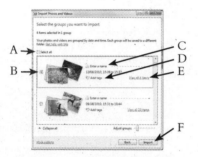

Fig. 12

- Click on the check box by **Select all** (A in Fig. 12) or remove the tick and then select just the groups (B) that you wish to import.
- Click on **Enter a name** (C) or **Add tags** (D) to type in your text if you wish to add names and tags.
- Clicking on **View all items** (E) allows you to review the photos in the group that you are importing.

- When you have made your selections, click on the **Import** button (F).

6. Whichever option you choose, the pictures are imported into Windows Live Photo Gallery.

7. Click on the link under **View your new photos** to view pictures that you have recently imported.

Section 12:
Edit your Photos in Windows Live Photo Gallery

1. Click on a picture that you wish to edit.

2. Click on **Fix** (A in Fig. 13) on the command bar.

3. Your picture is enlarged and on the right is the **Edit** pane (B) with editing tools. Click and drag the sliders to get the picture that you want.

Fig. 13

Tools on the Edit Pane:

Auto adjust: (C) use to automatically correct contrast, colour, brightness, tint and colour temperature.

Adjust exposure: (D) use to alter the brightness and contrast of a picture.

Adjust color: (E) adjust the picture colour.

Straighten photo: (F) use to straighten a photo.

Crop photo

1. Click on **Crop photo** (G).
2. A selection box (M) appears on the picture and the pointer changes into a four headed arrow.
3. Left-click within the box and drag the selection box to its new position.
4. Increase or reduce the size of the box by placing the pointer on any edge or corner. Click and drag the lines to whatever size you want.
5. Click on **Apply** (H).

Adjust detail: (I) use to adjust sharpness.

Fix red eye: (J) click and follow the instructions on screen.

Black and white effects: (K) experiment with filters.

Save your Photo Editing

Click on **Back to Gallery** (N) to save your edited image.

Redo, Undo and Revert

1. To undo or redo any editing, use the **Revert** and **Redo** (L) buttons at the foot of the editing pane.

2. If you have saved an image and later decide you wish to regain the original, click on the photo in the gallery.

3. Click on **Fix**.

4. Click on the **Revert** button.

5. Click on **Revert to Original**.

6. The original copy will be reloaded into the Windows Live Photo Gallery.

Note: when you revert to original any editing changes will be lost.

Section 13:
Publish your Photos Online

Window Live Photo Gallery enables you to share your photos online by publishing them on Flickr (a free photo sharing service provided by Yahoo!) or on Facebook, YouTube, etc.

1. Select the photos you wish to publish online.

2. Click on **Publish** (A in Fig. 14) and then on **More Services** (B) and then on **Publish on Flickr** (C).

3. Click on **Authorize** and you will then need to enter your Yahoo! ID and password to sign in. Once the Flickr website opens follow the screen prompts as they occur.

4. To publish on Facebook, YouYube and other photo blog sites click on **Add a plug-in** (D).

5. The **Windows Live Photo and Video Blog** (E) opens
in Internet Explorer.

6. Select which blog you wish to upload to and click on
the link.

7. Follow the onscreen prompts as they are displayed.

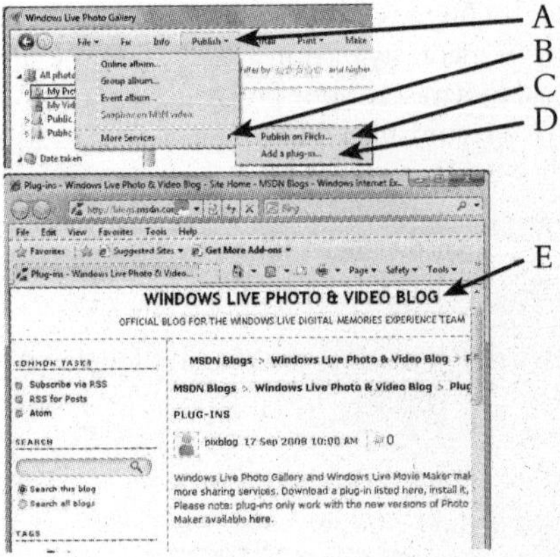

Fig. 14

Section 14:
Burning Photos or Videos onto a DVD

1. Open **Windows Live Photo Gallery**.

2. Select by clicking on the check boxes by each item, the
pictures or videos that you wish to place on the DVD.

3. Click on **Make** (A in Fig. 15) on the menu bar. Click on **Burn a DVD** (B).

4. **Windows DVD Maker** opens.

5. Use the tools to add or remove (A in Fig. 16), or rearrange (B) the order of the items.

6. Type in a name for the DVD (D).

7. Click on **Next** (C).

8. Select a menu style (B in Fig. 17) and use the options (A) to add interest to your DVD.

9. Insert a recordable DVD.

10. Click the **Burn** button (C).

Fig. 15

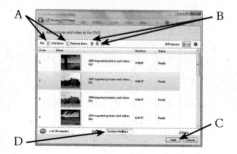

Fig. 16

Fig. 17

Section 15:
Using the Scanner

Importing Scanned Pictures into Windows Photo Gallery

1. Place the photo or image on the scanner bed.
2. Open Windows Live Photo Gallery.
3. Click on **File** and on the drop-down menu click on **Import from Camera or Scanner**.
4. On the **Import Photos and Videos** box, select the scanner that you wish to use.
5. If the name of your scanner is not listed, check it's properly connected and switched on. Click on the **Refresh** button.
6. Click on the **Import** button.

7. The **New Scan** dialog box opens. This allows you to select your preferences for the scanning settings (A in Fig. 18).

8. Use the slider controls to adjust the brightness and contrast (B) to your liking.

9. When you have finished choosing the settings click on the **Preview** button (C).

10. Check to see if the picture is as you wish. If not, change the settings until you are satisfied.

11. Click on **Scan** (D).

12. The Tag box is displayed, should you wish give a tag to your newly scanned photo or image.

13. Once you have typed in your tag, click on **Import**.

14. A new Explorer window opens showing the scanned picture with the date it was scanned.

15. If you wish, click and drag to a folder or double-click the image to open in Windows Live Photo Gallery.

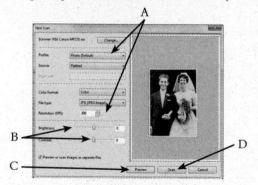

Fig. 18

Using the Scanner in Paint

1. Open **Paint** (if you have not used the Paint Program before see Chapter Nine, Section 3).

2. Click on the Paint button (A in Fig. 19), then click on **From scanner or camera** (B).

3. In the dialog box, click on an option button for the type of picture that you are scanning: colour, grayscale or black and white (C).

4. If you have an item which doesn't fit the normal settings, try using **Custom Settings** (E).

5. Click on the **Preview** button (G) to view the look of the image (D).

6. You can also adjust the appearance by clicking on **Adjust the quality of the scanned picture** (H).

7. The **Advanced Properties** box opens.

8. Once you have finished adjusting the settings, click on **OK**.

9. Click on the **Scan** button (F).

10. Once you have completed the scan, click on **Save**.

11. The Pictures **Save as** window opens.

12. Type in a name, select a destination folder and then click on **Save**.

*Note: you can use **Paint** to add text to your pictures and other effects.*

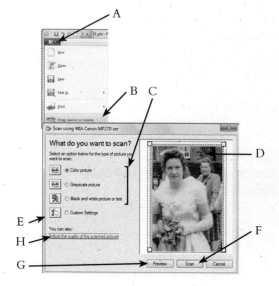

Fig. 19

Chapter Sixteen:
Entertainment

Windows 7 comes installed with two programs which enable you to work with your media files. Windows Media Player is a straightforward and utilitarian program which can be used immediately for playing and viewing CDs, DVDs and media files on your computer. Windows Media Center is a more versatile program but it does require various extensions to turn it into the fully flexible entertainment tool that it was designed to be. On a fundamental level both programs can do similar things and so it is up to the user to decide which they prefer to use.

Section 1:
Getting to Know Windows
Media Player

Windows Media Player is a program that enables you to play and download music, burn CDs and DVDs, create a media library and view pictures and video clips on your computer. Before you open the program make sure your computer is equipped with speakers or headphones.

Open Windows Media Player
1. Click on the Windows Media Player icon (A in Fig. 1) on the taskbar.
2. If it has become unpinned from the taskbar look on the Start menu.

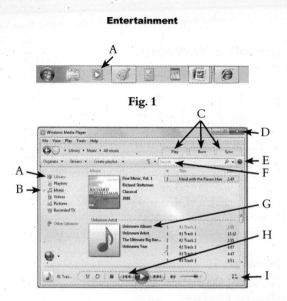

Fig. 1

Fig. 2

The Library

The Library (A in Fig. 2) allows you to organise music and other media that you store on your computer, and create your own personal playlists.

Click on Music (B), Videos, Pictures or Recorded TV to see Windows 7 samples displayed in the contents pane (G). Play, Burn and Sync tabs (C) are on the right of the library window. The Search box (F) lets you search for a media file within the library. Close Windows Media Player by clicking on the **Close** button (D).

Control Buttons

The playback controls (H in Fig. 2) sit at the bottom of Windows Media Player. Move your pointer over the individual controls to read an identification label for each.

Viewing Modes

Windows Media Player can be viewed in Mini-player mode, Windows mode and Full Screen mode. Look for the Switch mode icon (I in Fig. 2) to enable you to move easily between modes.

Updates

To get the latest Windows Media Player updates, click on **Help** on the menu bar and then on **Check for updates**. Alternatively, click on the Help question mark (E).

Section 2:
Playing Videos, Music and CDs/DVDs in Windows Media Player

Playing a Video Clip

Windows Media Player allows you to play video clips that you have downloaded from your camera or the Internet.

1. Open Windows Media Player library.
2. In the navigation pane click on **Videos** (A in Fig. 3).
3. In the contents pane find the video (B) you wish to view. Use the scroll bar (C) to see more.
4. Double-click on the video to open.
5. The video opens within the Media Player Window (D).

6. Move the mouse over the lower part of the Media Player window and the playback controls (E) are displayed – use to stop, pause, etc.

7. To switch windows, click on the **Switch to Library** icon (F).

8. Use the toggle button (G) to **View Full Screen** or **Exit Full Screen**.

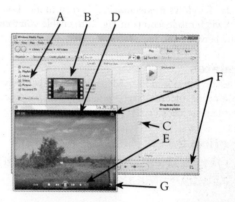

Fig. 3

Playing Music Saved to your Computer

1. Click on **Music** in the navigation pane.

2. In the contents pane, click on the album or track you wish to play.

3. Click the **Play** button on the controls.

4. Use the playback controls to choose the previous or next track, pause, play, stop and alter the volume.

Playing Music or Audio CD from the Desktop

You do not need to open Windows Media Player first in order to play a CD.

1. Place your CD into the correct drive.

2. The **Windows Media Player** mini-player window displays.

3. The music begins to play.

4. Use the playback controls to choose the previous or next track, pause, play, stop and alter the volume (C in Fig. 4).

5. If you wish to view the full Windows Media Player window and the music library click on the **Switch to Library** (B) icon. Note: the mini-player also has a rip button (A) – see Section 4.

Playing a DVD

1. Place the DVD into the correct drive for your computer.

2. The DVD will play automatically on Windows Media Player in full screen mode.

3. Move the mouse over the lower part of the window to view the playback controls.

4. Some DVDs have special features. If they are not displayed on screen, click on the down arrow to the right of **DVD** (A in Fig. 5) on the playback controls and select **Special features** (B) on the DVD menu options. You can also right-click on the window and another drop-down menu enables you to select more options and features for viewing.

Fig. 4

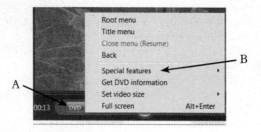

Fig. 5

Section 3:
Browsing the Windows Media
Guide and Listening to Radio Stations

1. Open **Windows Media Player** and connect to the Internet.

2. Click the downward-pointing arrow by the **Media Guide** button (D in Fig. 6) and then click **Media Guide** (E).

3. The Windows Media Guide will download.

4. Click on a word or picture link (A) to find out more information about a topic.

5. Use the control buttons (F) to adjust the sound, play, pause or stop a file.

6. The progress bar (G) will indicate the speed at which the file is being downloaded.

7. To listen to a radio station click on the link **Internet Radio** (A in Fig. 7) at the top of the Guide. Choose a country (B).

8. Choose your station. Click on the link **Listen** (D) below the station's name to hear the music.

9. To stop listening to a station click on the **Stop** button (E).

10. To search for more stations type its name into the Search box (C) and click the **Search** button.

11. Click on a stream speed (this is the speed at which the music is downloaded) – **Low** for a dial-up connection and **High** (F) if you have a faster Internet connection.

12. To close the Windows Media Player click on the **Close** button (B in Fig. 6).

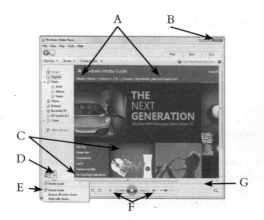

Fig. 6

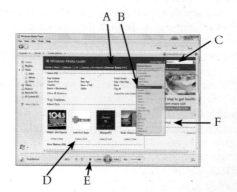

Fig. 7

Section 4:
Copying (Ripping) Music onto your Computer Using Windows Media Player

Copying music from a CD and storing it on your hard disk is called **Ripping**. You will need to abide by the current copyright laws where you live and those governing the music and the country where it was produced. In the UK check with copyrightservice.co.uk for up-to-date information.

1. Open **Windows Media Player**.
2. Insert the CD and the music starts to play.
3. Remove the ticks against the check boxes of the music you do not wish to copy (or click to add against those that you do) (C in Fig. 8).
4. If you know the format and audio quality that you wish to use, click on **Rip settings** (B) button and select the settings from the drop-down menu.
5. If you are leaving these settings unaltered, click on the **Rip CD** (A) button and the tracks are copied to the Music folder.
6. To stop the ripping process click on **Stop Rip**.

More Ripping Options
1. Click on the **Rip settings** button on the toolbar. Select **More Options**. The **Options** dialog box opens.
2. Select the options that you want by clicking the options buttons and check boxes that apply.
3. Click **Apply** and then **OK**.

Section 5:
Using Playlists in Windows
Media Player

To make your own individual collection of music tracks you can create playlists with different titles, incorporating your favourite tracks into any number of compilations. This is the quickest way to create your own playlist.

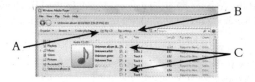

Fig. 8

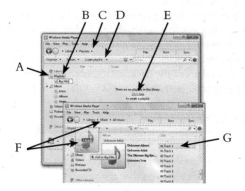

Fig. 9

1. Open **Windows Media Player**.
2. Click on **Playlists** (B in Fig. 9) in the navigation pane.
3. If this is the first time you have created a playlist, click on **Click here** (E) and then go to step 5.
4. If you wish to create a new playlist, click on the arrow (A) by **Playlist** in the navigation pane and then click on the **Create playlist** down arrow (D), and then click on **Create playlist**.
5. Type in a name for your playlist (C) and then press **Enter** to save.
6. Click on the **Music** Library.
7. Locate the tracks or albums that you wish to add to the playlist (G).
8. Click and drag music across the screen and release over the name of the playlist that you have just created (F).
9. Click the playlist to view its contents.

Viewing your Playlists

1. Click on **Playlists** (B in Fig. 9) in the navigation pane and the names of your playlists are shown in the contents pane.
2. To listen to all the tracks in the playlist click on it and then on the **Play** button.
3. To play an individual track double-click the playlist to view the music tracks in the contents pane.
4. Click on a track and then on the **Play** button.

Adding to Existing Playlists

1. Right-click a track or album and on the menu click on **Add to**.
2. Click on a playlist and the new item is added.

Deleting a Playlist

1. Locate the playlist in the navigation pane.
2. Right-click on it and from the drop-down list click on **Delete**.
3. Decide whether to delete from just the library or from the library and the computer, then click **OK**.

Section 6:
Burning a CD in Windows Media Player

Windows Media Player enables you to create CD copies of music from your computer, thus creating your own, customised compilations.

1. Insert a blank CD into your computer.
2. Click on the **Music** Library and then locate the items you wish to burn onto a CD/DVD.
3. Click on the **Burn** tab and the **Burn list** is displayed.
4. Click and drag music across the screen and release over **Drag items here** to create a burn list.
5. When you have completed the list click on the **Start burn** button.
6. When burning is completed the CD is ejected.

Section 7:
Browsing the Media Libraries in Windows Media Player

Windows 7 makes it easy to browse your media libraries.

Searching Using Categories and Columns

1. Open **Windows Media Player**.

2. Select **Music** from the Library button menu and a list of music is displayed.

3. On the navigation pane click on Artist, Album or Genre (A in Fig. 10) and the music will be grouped alphabetically (A–Z) in those categories.

4. Click on the **Album** *column* button (B) and the order will reversed to read Z–A. All the column buttons have this facility.

5. Experiment with the rest of the columns and categories in the navigation pane and discover how Windows Media Player works best for you.

6. Click on the **View options** button (C) to view in icons, tiles or details.

7. Use the Search box (D) if you cannot find the music you are looking for.

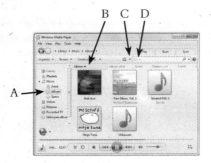

Fig. 10

Choosing Columns

Certain columns will open on Windows Media Player by default, but these can be changed according to your preference.

1. Click on a media library in the navigation pane.
2. Click on **View**, and then **Choose columns**.
3. Click on all the check boxes against the columns that you want to be visible. Then click **OK**.

Searching for Media Using the Search Box

1. Click on the type of media in the Library, i.e. **Music**, **Pictures**, etc.
2. Type into the Search box a word or phrase from the title of the work (B in Fig. 11). If you do not know the title, try the name of the composer or artist.
3. There is no need to press the Enter key as Windows Media Player will automatically search and display any matches (A).
4. Click on the artist's name to highlight all the tracks or click on an individual track and then click on the play button on the playback controls to play the music.

A   B

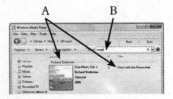

Fig. 11

Section 8:
Skins and Visualizations

Choosing a Skin

1. In Library view, click on **View** (A in Fig. 12) and on the drop-down menu click on **Skin chooser** (B).

2. Windows 7 comes with two styles: **Corporate** and **Revert**.

3. Click on a skin to see a preview.

4. Decide upon a style and then click on **Apply Skin**.

5. To download more skins, click on **More Skins**, which will take you online to the Windows Media website.

Fig. 12

Visualizations

These are patterns which are displayed on Windows Media Player while your music is playing.

To Change or Turn off a Visualization

1. Open Windows Media in Mini player mode (A in Fig. 13).

2. Right-click and from the drop-down list, highlight **Visualizations** (C).

3. Point to a category and then click on a visualization style (B).

4. To turn off the visualizations, click on **No visualization** (D).

Note: visualizations only play while music is playing.

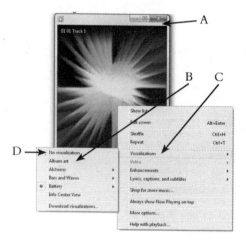

Fig. 13

Adjusting the Volume

1. Single-click on the sound icon on the taskbar (C in Fig. 14).
2. Click and drag the slider up and down to adjust the volume (A).
3. Click once on the mute button to mute the sound (B).
4. Don't forget you can also adjust the volume on your speakers.

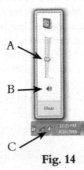

Fig. 14

Section 9:
Getting to Know Windows
Media Center

Windows Media Center enables you to watch live or recorded TV, listen to radio stations, play videos, music and games, play and burn CDs/DVDs, view your pictures and create slide shows. Before you can play radio or watch TV you need to connect to the Internet and install an FM tuner and a TV tuner card to connect you to cable or broadcast TV. To enjoy TV on your computer from an armchair you will also need a remote control or a wireless keyboard. Ask your local computer dealer or centre for help in adding these items.

Opening and Navigating Windows Media Center

1. To open, click the Start button, then on **All Programs** and click on **Windows Media Center**.

2. Use the up and down arrows on the keyboard to scroll through the main list of categories, which are: **Extras, Pictures and Videos, Music, Movies, TV** and **Tasks** (C in Fig. 15). You can also click on the down arrow (D) to move through the categories.

3. Use the left and right arrows on the keyboard to scroll through sub-categories (E).

4. Click on the **Back** (A) button to get back to the previous screen.

5. Click the **Home** (B) button to return to the main screen.

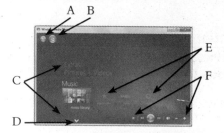

Fig. 15

6. Use action controls (A in Fig. 16) to play, restart, resume, delete or add to list.

7. Use the controls at the bottom of the screen to stop, pause, play and control volume (B).

Find Out More About Windows Media Center

1. To learn more about the Windows Media Center, click on **Help and Support** and in the address bar and type in **Media Center**. Windows Help and Support will display the best 30 results. Click on the first in the list which should be **Getting started with Windows Media Center**.

2. With the main screen on **Windows Media Center** open scroll down to Tasks, then scroll to the left and click on **learn more**. (You will need to be connected to the Internet.)

Section 10:
Play your Pictures, Videos and Slide Shows in Windows Media Center

1. On the main screen select **Pictures and Videos**.

2. To view a video uploaded onto your computer, click on **video library** (Windows 7 includes a sample video). For videos not included in a folder, click on **date taken** to list them – click to open.

3. To view uploaded pictures, click on **picture library**.

4. The screen displays your picture folders sorted by name. Click on the categories (B in Fig. 17) across the screen to sort by date, by rating, etc.

Fig. 16

Fig. 17

5. Click on a folder (A) to open, and then on a picture (C) to view.

6. Use the left and right keys to scroll through the pictures in a folder.

7. To create a slide show from a folder of pictures, click on the folder and then on **play slide show** (D).

Configuring Live TV

1. On the main screen, scroll to **TV** and then click on **live tv setup**.

2. Select your region and then click **Next**.

3. Enter your postal code, click **Next** and then accept the Microsoft licence agreement. Click **Next**.

4. The TV set-up wizard then takes you through the rest of the process. Click on **Finish** when completed.

Extras – Gaming

1. This category contains the Windows 7 games.

2. On the main screen select **Extras**.

3. Click on a game, select your options and then play.

4. To exit, click on **Exit Game** in the top left of the screen.

Section 11:
Playing Music in Windows
Media Center

1. On the main screen click on **Music**.

2. Click on **Music Library**. The Library will open with the music on your computer classified by albums. Click on the categories across the screen to select a different way to sort your music.

Fig. 18

3. Click on an album and then on **play album** on the actions list or on the playback controls at the bottom of the screen.

4. While the music is playing move your mouse over the left of the screen to view the various options available (A in Fig. 18).

5. Use the **Back** button (B) to get back to the Music Library.

6. To play music from a CD, insert the CD (if Windows Media Player opens, close it).

7. If Windows Media Center recognises the CD its title will appear in the Music Library – otherwise it will be listed as **unknown album**.

8. Click on it to view the tracks (D in Fig. 19).

9. To play all the music tracks click on **play album** (B). To play an individual track (C) click on a track name or number and the options change to **song details**. Click **play song**.

10. To stop or pause the music use the playback controls.
11. To remove the CD move your mouse over the left of the screen onto the options and click **Eject CD**.

Section 12:
Ripping or Copying Music with Windows Media Center

Fig. 19

1. Insert the CD. (Windows Media Player may open: click to close.)
2. Select **Music** from the main screen and click on **music library**.
3. Click on the album title. If you are already online, wait for a moment for Windows Media Center to recognise the album. If not, it will be listed as unknown album.
4. Click on **Rip CD** (A in Fig. 19).
5. A new window opens. Read the options, choose one and click on the relevant radio button for **Do not add copy**

protection to my music or **Add copy protection to my music**. Click **Next**.

6. Click to accept the licence agreement, then **Next** and then **Finish**.

7. Click **Yes** to **Are you sure you want to rip this CD to your Music Library?** The CD is then ripped to your hard drive. The tracks are listed, with the ones above the rip icon already ripped.

Section 13:
Windows Media Center Settings

1. On the main screen, scroll to **Tasks**.

2. Click on **settings** (A in Fig. 20) and then click (or use the keyboard arrows) on the type of setting you wish to alter: **General**, **TV**, **Pictures**, **Music**, **DVD**, **Start Menu and Extras**, **Extender** or **Media Libraries** (B).

3. Click the check boxes or option buttons for the settings that you want. Click on **Save** or **Cancel** (if displayed).

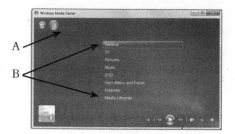

Fig. 20

Section 14:
Windows Media Center
Parental Controls

It's worth setting the parental controls on Windows Media Center before the computer enters family use and before set-up is completed. The process is the same whether the computer is used for just watching DVDs or TV.

1. Open **Windows Media Center**. Click on **Tasks**.
2. Click on **Settings**. Click on **General**. Click on **Parental Controls**.
3. Enter a four-digit access code (one that you will find easy to remember).
4. Click on **DVD Ratings**.
5. Click the check box by **Turn on movie blocking** and then **Block unrated movies**.
6. Use the plus or minus signs to select the highest movie rating that you wish to allow. Click on **Save**.
7. Click on the **Back** button and repeat this procedure for **TV ratings**. Click on **Save**.

Section 15:
Computer Games

Windows 7 comes with a number of computer games from Microsoft, collected together in **Games Explorer**. They are fun to play and simple to use.

Open Games Explorer and a Game

1. Click on the **Start** button, and then in the right pane click on **Games**.

2. **Games Explorer** displays the icons of those games installed on the computer.

3. Click on a game icon (F in Fig. 21) and the preview pane (D) (if not visible click on the preview pane button) shows rating, performance and score detail tabs (E).

4. Select a game to play and double-click on the icon (F). The game opens.

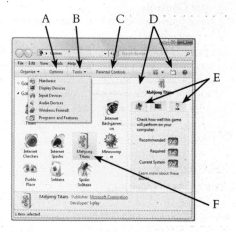

Fig. 21

Game Updates and Options, Software and Hardware

1. Click on **Options** (A in Fig. 21) on the Games Explorer toolbar.

2. Click the appropriate option button to check manually or automatically for game updates.

3. Click or clear the check boxes to download game art and information.

4. To access software and hardware that you may need to play some games that you add and install onto your computer, click on **Tools** (B) on the toolbar.

5. To get straight to parental controls click on the button **Parental Controls** (C).

Learn How to Play a Game and Adjust the Levels of Difficulty

1. Open Games Explorer and then double-click on the icon of the game that you wish to play.

2. To learn how to play and more about the game, click on **Help** (B in Fig. 22) on the game menu bar.

3. To alter the level of difficulty click on **Game** (A) on the game menu bar and then on **Options**.